Praise for *Letters to a Yo*

"[T]he letters stress the importance of having options and working smart, not just hard."
—*The New York Times*

"In clear, accessible language, Harper encourages his youthful readers to maintain productive values and never give up hope. . . . Harper helps young readers take that first step toward fruitful change."
—*The Washington Post*

"Harper's message is a solo soaring above the choir. . . ."
— *Los Angeles Times*

"Filled with heartfelt wisdom and solid step-by-step strategies for cultivating self-respect, *Letters to a Young Brother* is an inspirational guidebook to a better life and a book that will change lives."
—*Black College Today*

"Young men facing tough issues can find advice in Hill Harper's new book. . . . [It] can serve as a strong but silent mentor."
—*The Philadelphia Inquirer*

". . . an inspirational guidebook for young men. . . . [Harper] tackles real-life issues that young men encounter today."
—*The Charlotte Post*

"Not your average Hollywood hunk. . . . "
—*Jet* magazine

". . . a mentor with plenty of pearls of wisdom to share . . . [*Letters to a Young Brother*] is a priceless, no-nonsense, step-by-step guide out of the ghetto, provided it reaches a pair of receptive ears with a support team prepared to help him achieve his dream."
—*Black Entertainment*

"Harper infuses his words with a healthy dose of optimism as well as insights."
—*Black Issues Book Review*

KEITH MAJOR

Currently starring in *CSI:NY*, **Hill Harper** has appeared in numerous prime-time television shows and feature films, including *Beloved, Lackawanna Blues, He Got Game, Get on the Bus, The Skulls, In Too Deep, The Nephew,* and *The Visit*. He graduated magna cum laude with a B.A. from Brown University (and was valedictorian of his department) and cum laude with a J.D. from Harvard Law School; and he holds a master's degree in public administration from the Kennedy School of Government. He is also a volunteer for the Big Brothers Big Sisters organization in Los Angeles and is a motivational speaker at public schools around the country. Recently named one of *People* magazine's Sexiest Men Alive, he lives in Los Angeles.

HILL HARPER

Letters to a YOUNG BROTHER

𝕸𝖆𝖓𝖎𝖋𝖊𝖘𝖙 𝖄𝖔𝖚𝖗 𝕯𝖊𝖘𝖙𝖎𝖓𝖞

GOTHAM BOOKS

GOTHAM BOOKS
Published by Penguin Group (USA) Inc.
375 Hudson Street, New York, New York 10014, U.S.A.

Penguin Group (Canada), 90 Eglinton Avenue East, Suite 700, Toronto, Ontario, Canada M4P
2Y3 (a division of Pearson Penguin Canada Inc.); Penguin Books Ltd, 80 Strand, London
WC2R 0RL, England; Penguin Ireland, 25 St Stephen's Green, Dublin 2, Ireland (a division of
Penguin Books Ltd); Penguin Group (Australia), 250 Camberwell Road, Camberwell, Victoria
3124, Australia (a division of Pearson Australia Group Pty Ltd); Penguin Books India Pvt Ltd,
11 Community Centre, Panchsheel Park, New Delhi–110 017, India; Penguin Group (NZ),
67 Apollo Drive, Mairangi Bay, Albany, Auckland 1311, New Zealand (a division of Pearson
New Zealand Ltd); Penguin Books (South Africa) (Pty) Ltd, 24 Sturdee Avenue, Rosebank,
Johannesburg 2196, South Africa

Penguin Books Ltd, Registered Offices: 80 Strand, London WC2R 0RL, England

Published by Gotham Books, a division of Penguin Group (USA) Inc.

Previously published as a Gotham Books hardcover edition, May 2006

First trade paperback printing, April 2007

20 19 18 17 16 15 14

The Library of Congress has catalogued the hardcover edition of this book as follows:

Harper, Hill, 1973–
    Letters to a young brother / by Hill Harper.
        p. cm.
    ISBN 1-592-40200-3 (hardcover)   ISBN 978-1-592-40249-6 (paperback)
    1. Young men—conduct of life. I. Title.
    BJ1671.H35 2006
    170.84'21—dc22   2006003699

Printed in the United States of America
Set in Dante MT   Designed by Sabrina Bowers

MANifest Your Destiny

Contents

CONTENTS

Part Three

The Real Deal:
Girls, Sex, and Responsibility

Part Four

Dreams and Aspirations:
Making It Happen

Part Five

Winning at Your Life:
Setting Sail

One's sense of manhood must come from within.

—*Dr. Martin Luther King, Jr.*

Introduction

A number of years ago, someone gave me a copy of *Letters to a Young Poet* by Rainer Maria Rilke. He told me it would change my life and he was right. In it, Rilke responds to the questions of a young man who writes to him asking for advice. The inspirational messages for any young artist—or young person—are clear throughout the book. To this day I often reread many of its pages and have given the book as a gift countless times. The title, *Letters to a Young Poet,* as well as my experiences speaking with thousands of young people over the past few years, inspired me to write this book. In the way Rilke served as a mentor to the young poet who wrote to him, I hope to be a mentor to all of the young men I've been meeting and speaking to. In this book I hope to address many of the questions they've been asking me.

Letters to a Young Brother is a book I hope will inspire young men and affect positive change in their lives. So many young men today are lost. They *want* to be inspired, motivated, and guided—they are almost crying out for it—but often feel that they have nowhere to turn, no one who truly understands their world. Those who love them (parents, uncles/aunts, and family friends) often have trouble communicating with this video-game and music-video generation. So every time I have the opportunity to address young audiences—more than ten thousand middle school, high school, and college students over the past two years—I've gotten pleas from students, parents, and teachers alike for alternative ideas and goals to playing *Grand Theft Auto: San Andreas* and wearing platinum Rolexes.

Young men today have been bombarded with images of wealth and success that tell them that buying the "hottest" car or the most "bling-blingin'" jewelry is what they should be motivated by. There is an overwhelming sales pitch targeted at these young men that subliminally suggests that material goods are the extent of their birthright and are what make them become real men. I want young men to have knowledge of the things that bring them *true* empowerment: education, a strong sense of purpose, compassion, confidence, and humility, to name a few. Sadly, however, many young men are stuck in a system where they feel they can't get ahead. It is imperative to me that young men become aware of their options. Unfortunately, it isn't always easy for them to speak openly with their family, friends, and those around them. That's where I come in.

Looking back, I am so grateful for the individuals who contributed to my maturation into manhood. They were people who taught me through word and deed that the world offers all of us a myriad of equally difficult and wonderful choices. My teachers, coaches, parents, and grandparents insisted I could achieve anything I wanted. They taught me that my life was important and that I should not waste it living below my potential.

My grandfather on my mother's side, Harold E. Hill, was from Charleston, South Carolina. All of his grandchildren called him "Pop." He had thick glasses and a deep scratchy voice that sounded much like the late great actor Adolph Caesar. Pop educated himself during the 1920s and became a pharmacist. In 1936, he moved to Seneca, South Carolina, and opened Piedmont Pharmacy. It was the only pharmacy for miles where black people could fill their prescriptions and be treated equally. To his customers he was simply "Doc." As a boy, I remember sitting at the marble soda fountain in the pharmacy reading comic books, licking Popsicles, and watching him fill prescriptions one by one. He treated every person who walked through the door with love and respect, whether they could afford to pay for their medicine or not. When it was time to go home he would always say, "You want another Popsicle, boy? Go on. Grab one out of the cooler." He was a man of few words but infinite dignity.

My grandfather on my father's side was Harry D. Harper, Sr. All of his grandchildren called him "Father." He was the seventh of nine children; four boys, five girls. His dad worked for the public utility in Fort Madison, Iowa, and desperately wanted his children to get a higher education. All of them did that, and more. Since they couldn't afford to go at the same time, each sibling attended college in sequence. After one graduated, he or she would pay for the next sibling to attend college. Miraculously, during Jim Crow segregation, one by one, all four boys became doctors. My grandfather became a family practitioner and returned to his Iowa hometown. In the 1920s, Father set up a practice in a small shack near the railroad tracks in Fort Madison. The white-owned banks refused to allow him to open a savings account, so he literally had to keep the money he earned under his mattress. In 1928, when the stock market crashed, banks froze assets; people were fearful and needed money. Because of the banks' racism, my grandfather had access to his money. He reached under his mattress and, along with his brothers, purchased an apartment building that nearly spanned an entire city block in downtown Fort Madison. My grandfather and his brothers converted that building into a state-of-the-art medical clinic and lab with residential apartments above. For a number of years it became the number-one private medical practice in the state of Iowa. And for nearly forty years, until the end of Jim Crow, African-American women from four states would come and give birth in a safe, clean facility built for them and their families.

I saw both my grandfathers give of their expertise, oftentimes for free, or by trading medical services and goods for a turkey or crops when a patient had no money. Hero and legacy are two words that are often overused, but in the case of my grandfathers they could not be more appropriate. I couldn't be more proud that I am named after both of these great men. Through my memory of them I am reminded daily of the beautiful responsibility that being both a Hill and a Harper carries. I hope that as they look down on my life today, I have in some way made them proud. I cannot begin to imagine the difficulty my grandfathers faced almost eighty years ago. Whenever I feel I cannot accomplish something I remind myself, "If Pop (Doc Hill) and Father (Doc Harper) could make it happen, then Hill Harper can too."

The principle positive messages I received growing up were the examples my grandfathers offered me. Both of these strong men were passionate about their families and their work. They rose every day looking forward to what they were giving to the world. Each of my grandfathers taught me that there was value in contributing to my community. I grew up knowing that my grandfathers' jobs were equal in value because they each spent their lives in service to others.

Today, many young men lack strong male role models in their everyday lives. I hope that through the exchange of these letters I can be to young men what my grandfathers in their infinite wisdom were and continue to be to me.

Effective mentoring doesn't end with our blood relatives. For instance, a man who was not my blood relative, my uncle Russell who lived in Virginia, would call me every other month with his gruff voice asking, "You handlin' your business boy?" Which means, are you living up to your full potential in all the areas of your life in which you choose to participate? Obviously, when I was young that "area" was school, and his next question was always, "What are your grades?" I knew there had better not be one C on that report card and certainly no D or F grades. Uncle Russell did not even find Bs acceptable. He expected me to get all As and instilled in me an expectation of excellence, as if it was preordained that I would earn straight As. I believe that my desire not to let him down, as well as the confidence he gave me, contributed to me being an A student. The people in my life like Uncle Russell believed in me and in my ability to achieve success in any area of my life. It was as if their belief in me became the energy carrying me toward my destiny; whatever that destiny was to be. Whenever a relative, teacher, or mentor took that time to listen to me and educate me, they became one more person I could not bear to disappoint. Having people to believe in me, to mentor me, has been key in my development from boyhood to manhood.

I've learned that the trajectory of a young man's life results from many social and cultural forces. One of the most important of these is the adult men in his life. My grandfathers achieved prominence in their careers at a time when it was nearly impossible for black men to succeed. They set the bar extremely high for me, and at the same time awakened me to great possibilities for my future. It is no coincidence that both my mother and father became doctors just as it is no accident that I graduated from Brown University *magna cum laude* and received graduate degrees with honors from Harvard Law School and the John F. Kennedy School of Government. By going to college and graduate school, a whole new world was opened to me. My education gave me confidence and patience. If something wasn't going down the right track in my life, I had options because I could right myself and get back on track another way.

My family taught me that doing my best, educating myself, and being in service to others were not optional and that having values and being truthful were not negotiable. Through the letters in this book, I wish to pass on to other young men my grandfathers' legacies of education, hard work, determination, and success. I am living proof that these principles work. It is my hope that these letters will inspire other young men to live out their dreams. We are all completely unique manifestations of the human species, and the wonder of that gift provides all of us with an opportunity to reveal new and different ways to represent our fullest potential.

The "Young Brotha" in these letters is a compilation of hundreds of young men I've met over the past five years. His questions to me are all questions I have been asked numerous times by young men through letters, e-mails, and in person. It is with honor and gratitude that I am able to share these letters with numerous other young men who have their entire futures ahead of them and deserve the same guidance, support, and encouragement I received when I was their age.

Part One

You, Your Friends and Family: Building a Solid Foundation

MANifest Your Destiny

Young Brotha:
The Newest Perfect Model

. . . I'm not cocky, I'm confident
So when you tell me I'm the best it's a compliment.
JADAKISS
"NEW YORK"

April 9, 2005
Los Angeles

**ear Young Brotha,**

What's up man? So I got your letter. And as much as I hate to admit this, you are right. I probably would not have written you back. At least not so soon. I often fall into the trap of thinking I'm so crazy busy that I can unknowingly get bogged down with the daily business of life.

But, something in your letter, your vibe, your tone, caused me to stop and pay attention. It troubled me that at such an early age you already expect the worst from people. More than that, you remind me of myself at your age. Just like you, I had gotten used to people letting me down. At times, it even made it hard for me not to give up on myself. Your letter hit home with me, man. It forced me to remember what it was like to be a young man in need of things I couldn't always put into words. I know what it's like to be confronted with multiple roads you could choose to walk down; some positive, some negative. So, yeah, I'm doing what you said I wouldn't do. I'm writing you back, and there's so much I want to share with you.

First, I want to tell you something. You are the perfect product of 15 billion years of evolution. That means you are the latest and greatest model of the human species. I respect that, and you should too.

You know how cars come out each year and they make an upgraded improved model? You know how they make it look better, go faster, upgrade the engine, upgrade the sound system? Your grandfather's Cadillac went 0–60 in 8.2 seconds. The Caddys today go 0–60 in five seconds. His car had lap belts, no power steering, and skinny tires. Today's model comes fully equipped with front and side air bags, integrated traction control steering systems, and twenty-inch rims. You can't mess with the new model. It's hot. That's you, and I want you to hear this: You are the latest and greatest, perfect model of the human species . . .

> *You are the perfect product of 15 billion years of evolution.*

and each year you can improve. You can become the upgrade you are seeking.

The way you are right now, today, is perfect. I can't say it enough. This is the truth. You are the latest, newest model. Being younger than I, you can do stuff I can't do. You still have the time to get great grades in school, fall in love for the first time, and see the Eiffel Tower in France, the Serengeti in Africa, or the Aztec ruins in Mexico. You can even learn another language, or change careers, or do a myriad of things. You are still able to bring fresh new dreams into reality. I bet you could kill me at the latest video games too. I don't know how to play *Grand Theft Auto: San Andreas*. But, I'm not supposed to be able to beat you because I'm an older model. However, one thing that we've learned from car designers is that they always study past designs to get a vision for the future.

So let's stick with this car analogy, okay? Cool. What is your favorite new-model car now? That '06 model is hot. Yeah, it's better than the '04 model, which was better than the '02 model, but it's better because they improved on it. The '06 evolved from the '04, which evolved from the '02 and so on and so on and so on. That is why you are an improved version of almost everyone in your life. You're an improved version of your parents and their generation. You're an improved version of your grandparents and their generation. This doesn't mean you shouldn't respect them or that you're better than they are. And it certainly doesn't mean that there aren't many important life lessons that come from listening to and being interested in your parents' and grandparents' stories. However, it does mean you have your whole future ahead of you. You can learn from their mistakes and do better. You will live longer, become better educated, make more money, and be happier than the previous generation. You are here to improve the human race, and you need to embrace that. So, right now as you're reading this, whisper to yourself, "I am the perfect new model." "I'm going to do better than my parents." "I, today, am the best this world has to offer."

I know little seeds of doubt try to pop up when you imagine your best self. These little voices crop up saying, "No you're not the perfect new model." "You're not that good." "You're not gonna be happy." "You're not gonna be successful." "Who do you think you are?" "Life is tough and you suck." Tell those voices to get up off you. I say that because I, too, fight those voices in my head that tell me I can't be something or do something. They never fully go away, but doing this work can take those voices from a loud yell to a soft whisper. The most important thing to remember about those voices is that they are wrong. You are the newest perfect model. You are perfect, and you have all the potential in the world.

That voice of doubt is in your head because a previous model (a previous generation) taught you those limiting beliefs. You are not born with that voice of doubt. I am here to tell you that I am living proof that those voices of doubt aren't real; they are not even yours; and they don't belong to you. Someone taught you to believe in those doubts. Success, happiness, joy—these are your birthrights. You know what I'm sayin'? Let go of other people's voices in your head; your parents', your relatives', your friends', your enemies', anybody who ever said your dreams were not possible. Let it all go. I know it's easier said than done, but if you stick with me, I promise someday you will be unreasonably happy.

All right, I gotta go shoot a scene for my show, *CSI: NY*. It's a scene in Central Park where I go scuba diving to recover a body. Cool, huh? If I can, I'll grab a picture of me in the scuba suit and send it to you. If you write me back, I'll elaborate on doubt and the power of belief in another letter.

So hit me back and we'll rap some more. We got a lot

more to talk about. Okay? Oh, and feel free to shoot me an e-mail if you ever have a question. My e-mail address is: Hill@manifestyourdestiny.net. Hope to hear from you soon.

Grace, Peace, and Blessings Young Brotha.

Your Friend,

Hill

P.S. As I was finishing this letter to you, my friend Stephanie gave me this greeting card that on the front says, "You are the best invention since last year." It was written by a six-year-old boy. How's that for serendipity? It's the universe's way of showing us that this is the truth.

----------Original Message----------

From: Young_Brotha@home.net
Date: April 17, 2005 5:48 PM
To: Hill@manifestyourdestiny.net
Subject: Qualities

Hill,

What are the qualities of a good man?

Date: April 18, 2005 12:42 AM
From: Hill@manifestyourdestiny.net
To: Young_Brotha@home.net
Subject: Re: Qualities

A good man is honest, lives his life with integrity, and behaves responsibly. A good man loves God and his fellow humans on this Earth. Sometimes words like "macho" or "cool" are used to describe a "man," but truly being "macho" or "cool" means going anywhere with courage, integrity, and perseverance. All of those define a good man. A good man is not defined by what he has—be that money, cars, or girls. A good man is ultimately defined by what he does.

But I don't want you to have just my perspective so I forwarded your question to two men who I don't just consider "good men" but "great men." I asked my man Nas, a talented rapper, and Curtis Martin, one of the classiest guys in the NFL, to answer your question for you as well.

HH

----------Begin Forwarded Message----------

Dear Young Brotha:

Being a man is the greatest achievement—age doesn't do it. Knowledge and wisdom do. The young are very impressionable and sometimes need to belong to groups like gangs. But even that can become tiresome and you'll have to stand on ya own two one day, making ya own decisions. A man plays a major role in society and the world. And you can become that man, Young Brotha.

Nas

----------Begin Forwarded Message----------

Dear Young Brotha:

Be Balanced: secure enough to be vulnerable, strong enough to be gentle, wise enough to be humble, and powerful enough to serve others. Don't let the words of others stop you. Only fear God. Have a quiet confidence, faith, and belief that you can conquer whatever life may bring. Put God first, family second, and yourself third. Respect others, but remain true to yourself. And at the end of the day, know how to have fun and enjoy life!

Sincerely,
Curtis Martin

Friends as Family

*Lots of people want to ride with you in the limo, but what you want
is someone who will take the bus with you when the limo breaks down.*
OPRAH WINFREY

May 17, 2005
Los Angeles

Dear Young Brotha,

Hey man, it took you a while to write me back. I was hoping my first letter didn't scare you off or intimidate you. Glad to see it didn't. It's early morning here in L.A., and outside there's this kind of misty fog. (Or is it smog?) In your letter you kept saying, "I got things under control . . . on lock . . . I can handle things all by myself . . . I don't need anybody else." Everything you wrote, as well as your tone, concerns me—we all need help at different times in our lives, none of us can go it alone. That's why I'm writing you this letter.

First and foremost, I need you to know that you now have a new friend. I am your real flesh-and-bone, 24/7 friend.

Okay? Now, how do *you* define "friend"? For real, how do you define it? Write your definition of a friend on a piece of paper. I want you to do this because I was once told that if I can define what it is I need in a friend, I can allow someone to be that for me, and more importantly, I can learn to be that for myself. At first I thought it was bull, more grown-up overeducated crap meant to control how I felt and keep me out of trouble. But I was a know-it-all smart-ass ready to prove somebody wrong, so I gave it a shot. The first definition of friendship I came up with was: "A friend is someone I can whip all day at *Madden* and, he not only doesn't take it personally, he's up for a rematch the next day." Then it deepened for me, and I included words like loyalty, trust, and honesty. How you go about choosing your friends and the qualities that are important to you can impact you for a lifetime.

The reason I want you to define friendship clearly for yourself is because many times we have people in our lives who we call "friends," but they don't fit our description. They should be called acquaintances. When I was in high school I had a friend, Bobby, who considered himself something of a daredevil. He drove a bright red suped-up Ford Mustang that was the envy of all his friends, including me. Whenever Bobby had a carful of friends, he loved to punk people by driving recklessly. He would speed up and wait until the absolute last second before hitting the brakes and avoid slamming into another car. We all pretended to enjoy Bobby's thrill-seeking antics, but I don't think I was the only one who dreaded being in his passenger seat. One day, against my better judgment, I accepted a ride from Bobby.

It was what I thought would be a quick trip home. But Bobby drove in the opposite direction of my house, recklessly speeding up and slamming on the brakes for sport. After he narrowly missed the car in front of him that was carrying a mother and her two children, I became concerned for my safety and the safety of other drivers on the road. I didn't want to sit silently while Bobby put lives at risk. I told him to stop the car and let me out. I didn't get out of the car just for my own safety; I got out because I didn't want to validate Bobby's behavior. It didn't matter that it was the middle of winter, that we were nowhere near my house, or that I risked ridicule. He and the other guys cracked up. It was obvious that they didn't think I was cool.

As I stepped out of the car, I realized I was more than "cool" (and *cold*—it was freezing outside). They tried to tease me, but I couldn't care less. I was smart enough to see our appointment with tragedy if I kept getting in the car with Bobby, and I decided to avoid it. I realized then and there that my life was too valuable to cave to peer pressure by doing things I didn't feel were right just so that other people would think I was cool. To me, there was nothing cool about letting other people lead me down a road to trouble. And moreover, I realized that if I didn't speak up about other people's actions that I knew were wrong, then I was a silent accomplice in their actions.

The reason I'm telling you this story is to illustrate the importance of choosing your friendships based on

Pick friends that you wish were your family.

strong shared convictions. You can't pick your family, but you can pick your friends. So pick friends who you wish were your family. Today, I have a wealth of solid friendships, and by that, I mean people I can call in a pinch at three in the morning. Luckily for my friends, I haven't needed to make too many of those calls. But it's crucial for me to know I have friends who love me enough to be there for me no matter what. Shout out to all my friends who are like family to me. My boys like Andre, Ari, Brian, Jordan, and Sean. Choose your friends wisely because they are a reflection of who you are.

Whatever definition you just wrote of how you define a friend, that's what I commit to being for you, starting now. I, Hill Harper, am your new friend. Someone was there for me once when I needed a friend, and that friendship changed my life. I was never able to repay the debt of that friendship, but when I read your letter it became important to me to be that friend to you. That means taking the time, energy, and interest to care about you. I like what the great Michael Jordan says about friendship: "Friends are my heart and my ears." A friend is someone who has your back. A friend is someone to talk with. A friend is someone who cares about you. I am someone who has your back. Do you see what I'm saying?

While it is important to have friends, it's also important to realize that you, completely on your own, have to be able to make yourself happy. It is by making active choices in our lives that include friendships, careers, education, hobbies, family relationships, and other interests that we learn how to bring happiness into our lives. When I was your age, I didn't even know I could be happy—not happy because I got some new gear or because some girl liked me, but happy just because I woke up in the morning with a day ahead full of nothing but possibilities. I am here to tell you that happiness is your birthright but happiness is also yours to choose. Let's make that choice right now. One of the ways I do this is with mantras (a word or series of words that helps focus your mind and spirit on a particular thought or goal) that I say to myself sometimes. Let's do this together. Repeat after me.

Right now, say to yourself, "I believe I can be happy." Say this right now. Repeat, "I am happiest when I approach life from a place of positive energy, passion, and enthusiasm."

You now have a new older brother, a friend, a homey, and a confidant who cares for you, who is watching you, and who is watching out for you. It is my wish that you are happy and you have the life you deserve. And believe me, you deserve a great life. I want to see you become unreasonably happy. And you can. And you will. If it can happen for me, little Hill Harper from Iowa City, Iowa, it can happen for you. Believe that. It doesn't matter if you are from a huge, loving family or if you are totally alone; by reading this letter, you have just inherited a new family member. Someone committed to you thriving in your life, and that's me, Hill, your new older brother. And guess what? I love you! That's right, I am not afraid to admit this truth out loud. I'll say it again. I love you. Yeah man, I mean *you*. Muhammad Ali says, "When you're as great as I am, it's hard to be humble." And I am not humble about the fact that I love you, my Young Brotha. The sheer truth that you are a soul who has a body makes you worthy and deserving of love. By reading this letter you have joined my secret society. You have joined my family. I'm gonna help you to become unreasonably happy. So what do you think? Oh, you think I'm kidding? No. This is for real. Fo' Real.

Your life isn't like a video game; it's not a movie or a TV show. It's yours and yours alone. It's really happening. Right now. Every second, every day, counts. You can turn this life into whatever you truly want and are willing to have. You can be the one your friends brag about. You can be the difference you are seeking. You own your life, completely, totally, and fully; no one else does.

Man, I got a lot more stuff that I want to tell you about.

And remember, we can talk about anything you want. Ask me about anything and don't be afraid to ask me the tough questions. It's only through having the courage to ask tough questions of ourselves and others that we can reveal what's really going on. For instance, write me back and tell me about your relationship with your mom. I've noticed you've kind of avoided that subject up until now. In your last letter, you kind of mentioned your mom and then said "It's no big deal." Whenever I hear someone say "No big deal," it's a sign that it *is* a big deal.

So write me back and let me know what's really going on between you and your mom. Try not to let any voices censor you from being completely honest. You can trust me with the information. I promise. Hit me back as soon as you can. One.

Your Friend,

Hill

----------Original Message----------

From: Young_Brotha@home.net
Date: June 2, 2005 3:46 PM
To: Hill@manifestyourdestiny.net
Subject: My friends at school

Hey Hill, how come when I sit in the front of the classroom and ask questions, my boyz punk me and say I'm trying to be the teacher's pet?

Date: June 3, 2005 8:23 PM
From: Hill@manifestyourdestiny.net
To: Young_Brotha@home.net
Subject: Re: My friends at school

There is nothing wrong with striving to make something of yourself. What is happening is that you are breaking away from the socially accepted norm that your friends have created for you, and it's not making them happy. In fact, your desire to learn is pointing out their flaws and their insecurities in the classroom. Rather than focusing on becoming better students and working hard at working smart and *using* school to get ahead, they are wasting an opportunity. So it is up to you to decide what is more important: your friend's taunts, or knowing how to use school and make the best of this opportunity. A lot of times as our interests change—you're getting interested in school, and your friends are getting less interested in school—you may find that these friends become more like acquaintances, and you'll find other friends that you have more in common with.

There are a lot of cool dudes who were teased by their friends as they were coming up because they were committed to excellence and seemed different than those around them: Will Smith,

Kanye West, and Tiger Woods have all said they were teased at different times when they were young. Do not allow other people's ignorance to interfere with what you know you have to do in order to be unreasonably happy and successful in your life.

I also passed your question along to Anthony Anderson, someone who's been my friend for many years and is one of the funniest actors around. He's been in many great movies, including *Hustle and Flow*, *Barbershop*, *Kangaroo Jack*, *Big Momma's House*, and *Romeo Must Die*. I knew he would have some insight into this topic, here's what he had to say . . .

----------Begin Forwarded Message----------

Dear Young Brother,

My advice to you would be to pick which pet you wanna be and continue to ask your questions. Personally I would choose to be a lion. What better pet to be than the king of the jungle? And not too many people I know would choose to punk a lion. The lion is a natural born leader and king. And when did getting an education become uncool? Continue to ask your questions and give your answers because if you don't what will you learn. And trust me, those who "punked" you for doing so will be the "punks" in life for not doing so. Knowledge and education is power; the more you have, the more powerful you'll be. Now take that back to the jungle and be king!

Be a lion,
Anthony

HH

Being Raised by a Single Parent

My mother never gave up on me.
I messed up in school so much they were sending me home,
but my mother sent me right back.
DENZEL WASHINGTON

June 19, 2005
New York

Dear Young Brotha,

In my last letter, I asked you to trust me with your thoughts and feelings about your family situation. I'm proud that you showed the courage to be as honest as you were. I don't think it's any coincidence that I received your letter about the frustration of growing up without a father on Father's Day.

In many ways, your situation is similar to my own. I, too, was raised by a single parent, only it was my mother who was absent while my father raised me. Many a Mother's Day passed with me feeling the sting of what I perceived as rejection from my mother's abandoning me. What was I supposed to do with the Mother's Day cards they forced me to make at school? I could have mailed them to her, but I didn't. How could a parent leave a child? Or was it just me? I covered it up and played it off like I was too cool to need a mom, but the truth was I *did* need her. My mother's choice not to be there devastated me for a long time. It made me feel rejected, like I wasn't good enough. It made me question my worth, and I wondered if everyone who looked at me could see what she saw—that I was leave-able. I was angry, and at times that anger made me destructive. I felt cheated at not having the picture-perfect two-parent life I deserved. Yes, Brotha, I, too, was messed up, even though I did have a parent there who loved and believed in me.

Luckily, as I matured and got to know my mother, I came to realize that her leaving wasn't about me or a testament to my worth as a human being. In fact, none of her decisions were about me. Sure I suffered the fallout, but she didn't intentionally set out to affect my self-esteem or my life. I realized she didn't leave me; she left the situation she was in—a situation that at the time wasn't healthy for her, or me, for that matter. At first I didn't understand how she could have made that choice, but as I grew into manhood, and we strengthened our relationship, I came to a new understanding. That knowledge was key for me to building a healthy relationship with both my parents that lasted right up until my father passed away in 2000. Now, since my father isn't alive, the only remaining parent I have left is my mom. It's vital that I've developed a healthy understanding about her not raising me so that I don't resent her. Today I am able to have a healthy relationship with my only living parent. And family is so key.

Everyone's family life is different. Your situation differs because your father never tried to help your mother raise you, which happens too often when people have babies when they're still teenagers. Let me tell you a story about a friend whose father denied his paternity. That means his father refused to accept that he was my friend's father—he wouldn't accept that he had a son, and therefore wouldn't visit him or acknowledge him. And that hurt. One day, I asked him how he could stay so positive and seemingly unaffected by his father's denial. His response was, "Rejection is God's protection." He had finally met his father and dis-

Everyone's family life is different.

covered that the man he had dreamed would one day rescue him was the opposite of a warm, loving, welcoming father. He thinks if he had grown up with his father that he probably would have inherited his father's bitterness, cynicism, and unhappiness. My friend considers his upbringing by his single mother a far better alternative than a life with a man who would have never made him feel loved and accepted.

So the most important thing I learned is that my absentee parent didn't leave me, she left the situation. My mom left the relationship with my father because she felt she had no other choice. Even though your father may have left when you were a baby, it's important that you realize he didn't leave *you*. He didn't even know you. Your father left for reasons that had nothing to do with you. He may have been scared of the situation, and fear often makes people run away. Perhaps at the time, your father wasn't strong enough to handle his responsibility. But that's not a reason to resent him or be angry with him. He was doing the best he could, even if his best was not good enough for you. That's a reason to embrace him, to be more compassionate toward him, because like I said, "you are the newest perfect model" and you can handle things he can't. We need to learn to be the most compassionate toward those who are the weakest. It's important not to take people's humanness personally. As human beings we make many mistakes—mistakes that often affect those around us. It is also important to be able to forgive people, even if those people are your parents, so that you can have a healthy, happy life. I'll never forget the first time I came to understand that my parents were human beings (works in progress), as opposed to the superhuman Godlike creatures I believed them to be. It was a huge wake-up call that made me understand that parents are just people who are trying to do the best they can with what they have been given.

Sometimes things happen in your life that can cause you to question everything, especially the strength of your family's love for you. After my parents' divorce it was important to my father that he be the one to raise his two sons. Eventually, my brother and I ended up living with him. I will never forget the day my mom was visiting us at my dad's new house. I heard arguing, and I came out into the hallway just as the argument turned physical. I saw my mother crying as she leaned up against the wall. As a seven-year-old, witnessing my father's anger and my mother's tears made me painfully aware of my vulnerability. That one moment shattered my innocence. I felt like I didn't know these people at all. They were not the parents who had always nurtured and protected me. If two people who promised to love each other forever could turn so completely to hate, then how secure was I in their love? For a long time afterward, I retreated into myself, and I waited in fear for that next event that would rip apart the already tattered seams of my family life I had known. It was the first time I saw my parents as vulnerable, flawed individuals with their own set of problems who could not always protect me. As I began to see the world with different eyes that day, I learned to depend more on myself and less on my parents. I guess I saw that even though your family may love you, we are all individuals who must make our own way in the world separate from anyone—even our parents. And so it is up to us to make ourselves whole, complete, secure, and unreasonably happy.

As much as I was upset by my parents arguing, I was more affected by seeing my mother so vulnerable. She had always been a strong, proud woman. As I matured, I realized that even though my mother looked like a victim at that moment, it was only at the moment. The choices she made and the life she led assured me of that. At a time when segregation was still in full effect, and most women—let alone black women—didn't even think of going to college, my mother not only went to college, she went to graduate school and became one of the first African-American female anesthesiologists in this country. Dr. Marilyn Hill Harper is far from a victim. I'm proud of my mom, and I know that you are proud of yours too. Now see, that's another thing we have in common: Both of our mothers deserve to be loved and respected, especially by us.

You say you want to solve the problem of your mom having to be both mom and dad. But not every problem is immediately solvable. There are some things that you may spend your entire life working through. They don't always affect you every day or hold the same importance over time. It's like the break that occurred between my parents, which in certain ways still affects me to this day. I still struggle with male-female relationships, never going past a certain point of intimacy. My parents split before you were even born, and I still haven't solved all the issues around it, but it doesn't stop me from living passionately and being unreasonably happy. I am still working on this area of my life and allowing myself to be more open and trusting in my relationships. So it's okay to still have unresolved feelings about your dad. The most important thing is to keep them in perspective and trust that you will solve them over time. Be patient with yourself, your mom, and your dad.

Truth be told, two parents in the home who aren't happy together isn't necessarily better than having a single parent. For example, one of my best friends in the world, a dude named James, was raised by both parents. Throughout his entire childhood, his parents fought and yelled at each other every day. There was no peace in the house. To this day, he acknowledges that after his father left, the house became more peaceful, because the arguments stopped. Now, clearly, having a strong, healthy, two-parent family is the ideal, but I know so many people, including myself, that have been raised extremely well by a single parent. There is nothing wrong with that.

Also, you may not understand this now, but there are ways that being raised by just your mom can be beneficial. It's a deeper relationship that forms between a mother and son. It's a different kind of bond. Your mom has been forced to be both your mom and dad. Witnessing the daily struggles, whether financial, emotional, or physical, of your mom can give you a better understanding of women. Moreover, it teaches you how to respect all women because those girls you see at your school will eventually, years and years from now, becomes someone's mom. Just as you don't call your mom "bitch" or "ho," you shouldn't refer to any woman or girl in that way, no matter how old they are. Words have power, so use them accordingly and respect women.

In your letter, you told me that things at home aren't going the way you want them to go. It might seem easier to close your eyes and ears and act like you're just passing time. But you're not. Your life's not. It just isn't. It might seem easier to ignore the fact that the choices for your life are yours to make, but get this: Not making any choices is making a choice. Do you hear me? If you choose to do nothing, then you are making a choice. You're actively choosing to do nothing. No matter what you do or don't do, you are always making a choice, so why not make a choice to be active and win at your life? That means choosing to deal with what is going on in your life today. Choose

> *Be an active architect of your own life.*

to do the things that will make you happy; actively and passionately choose to do the things that will make those around you happy. Commit to being an active architect of your own life and to turning your dreams into reality. For me, that means waking up every morning, getting on my knees, thanking God for the blessing of another day, and whispering the commitment to live this day to its fullest. I commit to live fully each day, each minute, each second. One day at a time. If you make this kind of commitment on a daily basis, then eventually they will stack up to be a pretty awesome string of very cool seconds, minutes, and days and that can become an "unreasonably happy" lifetime.

Before I forget, I wanted you to know how proud I am of the way you used your patience in dealing with your mom. It couldn't have felt good to argue with her that day, but the fact that you walked away before it became too heated was admirable. The fact that you then went to a place where you could be alone and breathe was a sign that you are ready to change your life for the better. It's a sign that you are ready to be happy; to have the life you deserve. Maybe it was the first time you learned you could take a different approach to a problem. The goal next time is to stay calm and not allow things to get heated and escalate; calmly discuss issues with your mom from a place of love and respect.

Your mother is attempting to be both mother and father, just like my dad attempted to be father and mother to my brother and me. I remember him saying to me the reason why he got up every morning and cooked my brother and me a hot breakfast was because that was what his mom did for him. My father had very definite ideas about what a man is and how a man should behave. He had clear-cut expectations of my brother and me. I had chores and curfews, but my real job was school, where I was to be well-behaved and get good grades. My father was a perfectionist, and at times I found living up to his standards impossible. But I am so grateful that he taught me the value of discipline and hard work. He attended Howard University Medical School, the same college his father graduated from years earlier. So I knew that having strong expectations was a legacy he inherited from his father. It was one of the ways he learned how to be a strong parent to his sons. Still, it didn't make it any less painful or annoying when I didn't agree with his rules. So, go easy on your mom, she's doing her best I'm sure. Looking back, I have to admit that my father was usually right.

I truly understand your need for your missing parent. It's difficult to grow up without a strong male role model in your life. But let's you and me commit to becoming men our families can be proud of. I'm down for that, and I hope you are too. We have a lot more to talk about. I love getting those e-mail questions from you, so send me more when you get a minute. But right now, I have to get some shut-eye. I am being interviewed tomorrow for *The Early Show* on CBS. They call it that for a reason. So good night Young Brotha, I look forward to your next letter.

And, hey—do me a favor. Go up to your mom, give her a kiss on the cheek and wish her a Happy Father's Day.

Your Friend,

Hill

----------Original Message----------

From: Young_Brotha@home.net
Date: July 19, 2005 7:21 PM
To: Hill@manifestyourdestiny.net
Subject: Talking to my father

Hill, why is talking to my mother so much easier than talking to my father?

Date: July 20, 2005 10:42 AM
From: Hill@manifestyourdestiny.net
To: Young_Brotha@home.net
Subject: Re: Talking to my father

Before my father passed away, it was often very difficult to talk with him because I thought he might judge me harshly. There would be times when we had to take long trips in the car, and we might say two words between us. It wasn't as if we were mad at each other or anything. It's just I don't think he really knew what to say to me all the time, and I didn't know what to say to him. Our moms can sometimes have a more nurturing and accepting demeanor toward us, but that doesn't mean that our fathers love us any less. My father fiercely wanted what was best for me, and I'm sure yours does too. He just probably doesn't know how to express it very well. So the best thing I did was to try to figure out the things my father and I had in common. For instance, we both loved football and that was something we could talk about for hours and watch games together on Sunday. As you mature, you will find that your parents become more your friends than just your "folks." That is when your relationship will truly blossom. In the meantime, just keep being that newest, perfect model that you are, and reach out to your dad whenever you can.

Oh, and by the way, do you realize that today is the anniversary of the first time a man stepped on the moon? This day about forty years ago a dude named Neil Armstrong stepped off the lunar module, and as he was about to walk onto the moon's surface he said, "One small step for a MAN, One giant leap for MANkind." And you—your entire generation—are the "mankind" he was talking about. A guy has been on the moon. Forty years ago. This means one thing. You can dream about doing anything.

HH

Part Two

School, Work,
and Money:
Mining Our Resources

MANifest Your Destiny

Staying in the Game:
The Debt Rule

Too many people spend money they haven't earned,
to buy things they don't want, to impress people they don't like.
WILL SMITH

July 26, 2005
Los Angeles

Dear Young Brotha,

Hey man, I'm writing you from my house in L.A. I just got finished watching this documentary about the history of the U.S. military. I bet you probably knew this already (I didn't) but almost sixty years ago today, U.S. president Truman signed Executive Order 9981 to integrate the U.S. military. That's a huge step in the history of our country, and many historians think that the integration of the military led to the end of Jim Crow segregation about ten years later. History is cool isn't it? There's lots of things we can learn from our past, as we look ahead to our future. And speaking of future, today I want to write to you about *your* future. I want to write about something I call, "staying in the game."

There is only one way to be able to dream big, work hard, and achieve the goals that ultimately make you happy, and that is by "staying in the game." Yes, "THE GAME," and no, I am not talking about the rapper, but where do you think he got his name from? From this idea: "You got to be in THE GAME to win THE GAME." And the key to staying in the game is education.

In your last letter, you mentioned you were having trouble with school. You said you didn't like it because you didn't feel you were any good at learning. I want to help you shift your whole thought process about school. From what you said in your letter, you seem to think school is controlling your life. You are not alone. That's what a lot of young brothas think. What you don't realize is that school does not control you. *You* control school. Yes, I'm serious. You run school. Schools stay open because of your attendance. School is there to serve you, not for you to serve it. That being the case, you control it. I want you to start approaching your education from that place of power.

Since the key to staying in the game is education, it is essential that you take control of your relationship with school. Here's the deal, and this is for real: School, as hard as it may seem, is easier than the real world, and I'm not talking about the show on MTV. I'm talking about the real world where you've got to pay rent, you've got to buy food, you've got to get around, and you've got to be at your job on time and answer to somebody. Or if you choose not to have a job, then you've got to live with no money in your pocket—unless you choose to get involved in illegal activity, which then leads to a whole other set of very difficult circumstances. A lot of incarcerated brothas suddenly get interested in education and try to get their diplomas or college degrees in prison. Imagine how many of them wish they had stayed in the game when they had the chance. Once you leave school, you probably won't go back. I know that a lot of people say, "Look I'm going to take some time away. I'm gonna do this or do that, and then I'm gonna come back to school." You know what? Let's be real. They won't. Staying in the game could have changed their lives and put them on the path of success and happiness instead of lockdowns, curfews, visiting hours, and obstructed views of the sun. So, what I'm saying is that school, whether it is middle school, high school, or college, is much easier than the real world.

So what does that mean? That means we should stay in school as long as we can. I'm not saying it's easy or that everybody's experience is the same, but it is your responsibility to handle your business while you're in school. I know you said your math teacher seemed frustrated with you for having her explain an answer over and over, but it's great that you had her do that. You needed to understand the equation. That's you controlling school. You got the chance to practice not taking things personally. If you had, it would have taken you off the track of your getting what you wanted. In this case, you needed to understand the equation, and you did. Well done. You will find scenarios like that will be repeated many times in your life, and if you stay focused on what your needs are and don't let your ego take you off track, you will usually get what you are after.

Even if you have a teacher who believes you should study auto repair instead of calculus, it is your job to make sure that you learn calculus. By controlling school I mean getting your needs met; making the teachers do what they are supposed to do. If you don't understand something, then get them to give you a tutor until you do understand, or ask a teacher for help after class. Our brains don't all work at the same pace, so sometimes it's your job to help the teachers help you. Are you afraid your friends are gonna think you're weak if you ask questions or admit you don't know something? The great Muhammad Ali said, "I try to learn as much as I can because I know nothing compared to what I need to know." Be smart, know what you don't know, and do not be afraid to learn it.

> School is there to serve you.

A lot of young brothas say to me, "I can't afford to go to college because it runs up debt. I've got to get loans." Would you rather live your life in debt hustling in some dead-end job with little potential or would you rather be in school debt where you can get a good job and learn things that will help you forever? Debt in school is okay. And you will be able to pay it off because college will give you the tools to help you get a better job. Now, you'll hear me say this later, but there are only two areas where I think you should allow yourself to be in financial debt. When I say "debt" I mean owing someone else money that they will want paid back. The only two areas in your life where you should allow yourself to owe someone else money is for school (education debt) and when you buy your house—and notice I'm saying "when" you buy your house not "if"—that's what we call "mortgage debt."

To buy a house you don't need all the money. The bank gives you the money, which is called a "mortgage," and the only money you put up at the beginning is called the "down payment." Then the bank pays the seller of the house the rest of the money, and that difference is the "mortgage debt."

School debt and mortgage debt are the only two debts allowed if you are gonna hang with me and be unreasonably happy, like your big brotha, me! So you're not allowed to owe money to Little Jay on the corner; you're not allowed to owe money to car-dealer Carmine at the used car lot when you buy your new whip. There are only two areas of acceptable debt. That's the Debt Rule. Derek Bok, who is a professor and former president at Harvard University, has this saying that I agree with: "If you think education is expensive, try ignorance." Now, none of my posse is allowed to be ignorant, so we gonna get edu-ma-cated! Cool? And that's where the Debt Rule might come in to play.

Now, there's nothing wrong with having a new whip, but if you can't afford to pay cash for it and own it outright, then you would have to go into debt to own it, and that's not acceptable under the debt rule plan we're initiatin', right! That means when you buy a car you should buy a car you can "afford," and like my pastor used to say, "The car you can 'afford' may actually mean 'a Ford.'" Now me, I have a beautiful mint condition vintage 1959 Corvette. It was my dream car, fast and furious, and a car like that isn't cheap. But I applied my "Debt Rule" and bought it only when I could buy it without going into debt to own it. All cash baby. You will achieve that and much more if you follow what I say about staying in the game.

On the flip side, I personally know a lot about debt. Don't think just because I have money today that I haven't been in debt before. Why do I know debt? In order for me to afford college, and graduate school, I had to run up SEVENTY-FIVE THOUSAND DOLLARS in DEBT. Now let me repeat that: $75,000 dollars in school loans and student loan debt. $75,000! That was all on me.

I went to public elementary school, public middle school,

and public high school. When I went to college and graduate school it cost money, and I had to pay for it, but it was so worth it. Student loans and mortgages give lower interest rates and can be paid back over a long time. Both are like someone giving you money to fulfill your dreams. They are a blessing, and we all deserve the opportunity for a good education.

Something else also happened while I was in college that helped me. I received the Alfred T. Sloan Fellowship, which meant I got extra money to help pay for school. God truly does help those who help themselves. Now was it a good investment? Was I smart in running up that debt? The answer is yes. Absolutely. That investment has paid me back one hundred times over and not just in money terms. Ya hear me? Running up $75,000 in education debt was a smart move. Staying in the game was a smart move for me because it allowed me to figure out what I was passionate about in life. At Brown University I was able to take classes in philosophy, economics, political science, archeology, psychology, acting, urban planning, foreign languages, and sociology. Some of the subjects I liked; some I didn't, but it was only through exploration that I discovered my interests. I was even able to play football in college. I got to do it all while I was still figuring out what I wanted to do for the rest of my life! It's only through exploration and education that you can figure out what you really enjoy. Bill Cosby, who has earned nearly eight hundred million dollars over the course of his career, had a great quote about this very thing: "If I didn't work hard and make good at Temple University, I knew a lifetime as a busboy or a factory worker waited for me." What will make your life whole? What will make your life better and allow for you to: Be happier. Smile more. Love harder. Dream bigger. Achieve things beyond your wildest imagination. What?

When I say "education" I don't just mean traditional school—books and the classroom. Education can come in all shapes, forms, sizes, and ways. You may meet somebody who is gifted at doing something that you are interested in doing. You can approach them and say, "Can I volunteer to work with you?" Now, in the old days they called this an apprentice. There is a show on TV called *The Apprentice* about people working with Donald Trump, learning how to be successful in their fields. That's one form of education. I believe that if you want to be good at something, find someone who does the thing you want to learn or need to learn and ask them to show you—to mentor you. You can even have a nonverbal mentor by learning from someone simply through observing them. I did that with Denzel Washington. When we were shooting the movie *He Got Game* together, I would observe how he approached acting in scenes. I would observe how he rehearsed, how he interacted with the crew and with Spike Lee, the director. I was also interested in learning the process he went through to build his character in the film and the disciplined approach he took in preparation. There was so much I was able to learn from him without him having to walk over to me and say, "Hill, I am going to mentor you today." He "educated" me by example.

One thing I have learned about education is that there is a direct correlation between passion and skill. Luis, who is one of the mechanics on the MTV show *Pimp My Ride*, says that he got passionate about working on cars after he started to understand how all the different parts of a car work together. He learned from watching older guys work on cars and asking them questions about how each car part worked. Obviously, that's learning outside the classroom, and it has led to his success in that field. In today's world there are a million different ways to learn, especially with the Internet, which puts new technology and information virtually at our fingertips. Even if you don't own a computer you can get online at your local library and start exploring things that might interest you. Being around at this time in history affords us a huge opportunity. Technology can level the playing field for all of us, and that is something to get excited about!

It doesn't matter how much money you have or don't have; education is there for your benefit. For example, yesterday, I went with my friend Nichole to her Uncle Grady's funeral. We both felt a debt of gratitude to Uncle Grady, and I was proud I had stayed in touch with him over the years. Uncle Grady worked all his life as a cook at a local diner. He had to drop out of school in the tenth grade to support his younger brothers and sisters after his father was killed. But that didn't stop him from learning. For someone with so little formal education, he had an extensive book collection. He loved to learn and constantly told Nichole and me and any other child within earshot that education was the key to a better life.

Uncle Grady taught himself, but he originally wanted to go to college and become a teacher. He figured he'd have his chance after his brother and two sisters graduated, but by that time he felt too old and too responsible for his mom to leave her. His private dream became a public campaign to get all the children in his family and all their friends to attend college. He assured the reluctant ones that even an associate's degree from a junior college would be a great help in life as well as in getting a job. He searched for scholarship information for those interested in college. He helped out with spending money for college students, sometimes as many as ten at one time. Uncle Grady was a determined man, and I know he wanted to see me get an education. I wanted to make him proud, and I think I did. And, I want *you* to make *me* proud and that means—you getting an education. Ya dig?

I was talking to Kanye West the other day, and he said the same thing I'm talking about. He said: "Use school. Don't let school use you." You know what? He's absolutely right. What's key is to "Use school," which means stay in the game. Get education to work for you. Use it. It's a resource. It's a tool.

Hey, I got to run. I can't wait to hear back from you because in the next letter we need to discuss how running up a bunch of debt in school does us absolutely no good if we don't know how to "work hard" and more importantly "work smart." I know that sounds strange, but we'll have to discuss it later because right now I got to go. I have to go to a fundraiser for the NAACP's new president, Bruce Gordon. I hear he's a pretty cool guy.

> *"Use school. Don't let school use you."*

Remember, *you* control school. You got that? Hit me back. Let me know we're on the same page. Alright? Grace, Peace, and Blessings. Out.

Your Friend,

Hill

From: Young_Brotha@home.net
Date: August 3, 2005 3:18 PM
To: Hill@manifestyourdestiny.net
Subject: Tests

Hill, I want to go to a good college, but I'm no good at taking tests. What should I do?

Date: August 3, 2005 4:22 PM
From: Hill@manifestyourdestiny.net
To: Young_Brotha@home.net
Subject: Re: Tests

Hey man, first of all, you need to know that no one is born "good" at taking tests. It is a learned skill like riding a bicycle or playing a piano. Someone has to teach you the skill and then you have to practice and practice in order to get better. There are businesses set up just to teach test-taking skills. These are expensive, but many of them give grants to kids from families without a lot of income. Also, there are old test materials available for free in libraries and some of them can even be bought cheaply. Your school may have old SATs that you can use for practice. After you master the content and subject, you must practice, practice, practice. I was never good at taking tests, but when I found out that you could learn how to master standardized test-taking, I learned that every SAT test was pretty much the same format, and all they did was just change the facts in the questions. So once you master one, you've mastered them all. I went from being a horrible test-taker to scoring in the top 97th percentile in the country because I practiced taking tests. It was a lot of hard work, but so worth it. And you can do it too!

HH

Effort: Working Hard at Working Smart

*You've got to start with a plan. When I was in school, I took architectural
drafting and that taught me that everything starts with a plan. The biggest
buildings in the world start with a plan. You've got to have determination,
the talent, and you have to recognize opportunities and seize the moment.*

ICE CUBE

August 6, 2005
Cape Town, South Africa

Dear Young Brotha,

I'm down here in South Africa making a movie. We have
about four months off from *CSI: NY* before we go back to
shooting Season Two. I love to travel almost as much as I love
acting. Working on this movie, I am getting to do both at the
same time. I was blessed to get a job on a movie shooting in
South Africa, a place I've always wanted to visit. The people
are incredible, so generous and giving of their time and spirit.
Being offered this movie proves what I've been saying in these
letters to you: God and the universe will conspire to give you
what you go after as long as you are clear on what you want
and work hard for it.

Man, I was so happy to get another letter from you. Congratulations on that B+ in math and congratulate yourself for sticking with it. That is you controlling school. I already see that I'm going to have to sprint to keep up with you. Your questions are getting harder and harder.

Now, in my letter to you a few months ago, do you remember me writing something like: Dreaming big and working hard are the keys to maximizing the perfect model that you are. You remember that, right? Well you understood it because you wrote back: "How come everyone is always telling me to 'work hard, work hard'. . . . What is that anyway?" Now, in this letter, I'm gonna explain it to you. You ready?

The idea of "hard work" is something that people talk about all the time, but oftentimes they are never specific about what "hard work" really means. Colin Powell became the highest ranking officer in the U.S. military. He was the first African-American to rise to such a powerful position. He credits much of his success to "hard work." And with this quote he shows that "hard work" alone isn't the only component for success. He said, "There are no secrets to success. It is the result of preparation, hard work, and learning from failure."

When most people say "I work hard," what they really should be saying is "I work smart." There is a big difference between the two. You don't want to spend your life like a mouse on a treadmill running in a circle and never getting any farther. Like the Colin Powell quote above, "preparation" and "learning from failure" are the "working smart" components that need to be coupled with hard work to maximize success in whatever you do. What we want to work hard at most is working smart. Now, that may sound weird, but I'll say it again—we need to work hard at working smart.

"Working smart" means using your brain first to formulate

a plan of how to "work" most effectively. If you are working smart, you are first very clear about what you want to achieve—that's your goal. Then, before you take the first step toward achieving that goal, you use all the knowledge and information you have at your disposal to decide what the most effective route will be to get there. Now, there are always different means to achieving the same goal, but you "working smart" is *you* figuring out what would be most effective for *you*. For instance, I have to memorize a lot of dialogue when I do a play, or act on my show. I found that I memorize most effectively by writing the dialogue I have to say on a piece of paper. For some reason, writing them out helps me memorize my lines. But I know many other actors that memorize their lines by repeating them over and over. If I did it that way, I wouldn't be "working smart" for *me*. Your techniques of how you figure out how to work smart are specific to you.

Now I know you might be hearing that little voice of doubt popping up again: "How can I work hard at working smart when I don't think I'm really that smart in the first place?" I'm gonna remind you again that you are the latest model of evolution. You are the perfect model. You are better equipped to "work smart" than Einstein was. Einstein was a couple of generations ago; he was an old model. Einstein wouldn't know how to research and "Google" information electronically; he wouldn't know how to create an e-mail link within a text message or how to get money out of an ATM.

Einstein wouldn't even know how to make a Slurpee, or how to buy a Metrocard and get through the turnstile on today's subway, or how to pay for gas at an automatic pump. He would stand there confused wondering, "What do I do?" You know how to do all of these things because you are the newer, better model. Your grasp of technology and access to the information superhighway is far greater than that of any previous generation of people, including Einstein and even me.

The reason you will be good at working hard and working smart is that you are smart! Got that? But, "work" is still required to maximize your incredible potential. In order to work hard at working smart you need to figure out, analyze, and take a look at what the keys are to opening the doors that will eventually lead you to the goals that you want to achieve. In video game terms, it's the steps you have to take to go to the next level. Or even if you're battling somebody playing *NBA Live '06*, you're actively figuring out what your opponent's weaknesses are and manipulating them to score more points because your strengths are better than their weaknesses in the game. Feel Me? But to develop your strengths, you need what? Say it with me: ed-u-ca-tion. That's working hard at working smart. There is no shortcut to this.

You are a genius in training. Know this simple truth. When asked how he created his famous statue *David*, Michelangelo explained, "David was already alive in the marble, all I did with my chisel was remove the parts that were not David." You are a David, a masterpiece waiting to be revealed to the world. There doesn't have to be any

> *You are a genius in training.*

limit to your ambition. Your talent (being the newest and greatest model) is your ability to learn. So let's try another mantra. Whisper this to yourself real quick, "My talent is my ability to learn." Whisper it again.

Okay, write down some of the areas where you know you have talent. Go ahead. Even the things you believe you can do that others doubt—in fact write those first. Don't let that little voice of doubt stop you. Just do it! Are you good at communicating? Or are you good at analyzing a situation and knowing what to do next? Are you good at music? Reading? Science? Math? Puzzles? Poetry? Writing? Drawing? Computers? Do you have a good memory? If you really think about it, you are probably good at many things. And the best part of answering these questions for yourself is that over the course of your life, if you stay open to new things, you will discover that you are good at things that you didn't even know about. For instance, for me, it wasn't until college that I discovered I was good at acting, and it has become my life's work. And I just recently found out I was good at construction work. . . . Who knew?

Have you ever heard the phrase, "the world is your oyster"? What they mean by that is that anything in life you put your mind to, you can do. The only thing that can hinder you from being able to move through the world and make it "your oyster" is if your movement gets limited. For too many people, that means getting incarcerated. Incarceration (going to prison) is the only thing that can happen to you that could stop you from moving through the world to make it yours. Now, in prison, you can still learn, but you can't physically maneuver through the world to make the changes that you need and want to make. In video game terms, when you're in prison you're stuck at one level and no matter how good you get at playing the game, you can't go to the next one.

Kanye West also told me something that applies here. He said, "Do what you do to the fullest. Live your life, and be happy." Sound familiar? That's what we've been talking about. When I talk about education; when I talk about hard work; when I talk about dreams and goals; or even you talking to a cute girl, I'm not talking about something that's burdensome; something that's trying to make you feel like,

"Damn, I can't do it anymore"; something that's so hard it's dragging you down and making you tired. What I'm talking about is being happy! Smiling! Laughing! Having Fun! Crazy Fun! Just like Kanye said, "Do what you do to the fullest," which means: Work hard. "Live your life," which means: Work smart. "And be happy," which means: Smile and laugh because you are achieving your goals.

Well, they're calling me back to the set. This movie is called *The Breed*, and it's about five people on a deserted island who end up being attacked by killer dogs. And one of the damn dogs almost bit me yesterday!

All right, that's all for now. Hit me back and SMILE.

Your Friend,

Hill

----------Original Message----------

From: Young_Brotha@home.net
Date: August 18, 2005 8:13 PM
To: Hill@manifestyourdestiny.net
Subject: Mentors

Hill, you said in your letter to me I can do anything I want to do in this lifetime. My parents barely graduated high school. What makes you think I can run my own company one day? I don't know anybody who runs a big business. How can I even start to achieve that goal?

Date: August 19, 2005 9:57 AM
From: Hill@manifestyourdestiny.net
To: Young_Brotha@home.net
Subject: Re: Mentors

The reason I think you can do something like that is because there are other people who have already done it. Searching the web, you can find examples of men who have blazed that trail. You can use these examples as mentors in your life's journey. A mentor can be someone older or more experienced who helps you in your life and teaches you by example. This can be a teacher or a coach or someone you work for. But if you don't have a "real life" mentor, you can still look to people who have achieved great things and study them whether in books or on the Internet—or TV or movies to see how they achieved their dreams. By example, they can become your mentor, even if you don't know them.

I want to talk to you about three of the most powerful businessmen in the world. They also happen to be African-American businessmen: Stanley O'Neal, CEO of Merrill Lynch, a 1.5-trillion-dollar company, Ken Chenault, CEO of American Express, a 19-

billion-dollar company, and Richard Parsons, CEO of AOL Time Warner, a company with 6.9 billion in cash, not including its various companies. Stanley O'Neal was the grandson of a slave, and started out as a foreman at the GM plant in Detroit and didn't enter the financial world until he was thirty-six years old. All three of these men triumphed over great odds to rise to the top of major Fortune 500 companies. In Richard Parsons own words, "I always knew I'd rise to the top; it never occurred to me I couldn't." He embodies many of the principles I've been writing to you about and that you have been putting into practice. A great quote from Stanley O'Neal is, "I think life is about doing the best that you can with what you are born into. It's a fascinating journey to discover what that is." This quote comes from a man who grew up in the Jim Crow South and at one time picked cotton for a living. Ken Chenault gave a talk on leadership and integrity and one of the things he spoke of resonated for me: "If you are not clear who you are, or what it is you stand for, and if you don't have strong values, you are going to run your career off a cliff." These men are great examples for you and me. Each has created opportunities by pursuing their dreams. And moreover, there are tons of different careers out there that you can choose from.

I have also forwarded your question to one of the great mentors I have had in my life. Professor Charles Ogletree was my advisor when I was at Harvard Law School. He is a man that inspires me to continuously strive to be a better man and I think he could give some great insight into answering your question.

HH

---------Begin Forwarded Message----------

My Dear Brother:

My former student at Harvard Law School and friend, Hill Harper, has forwarded me your thoughtful question. Although I'm fifty-three years old now, the question you raised is one that I raised about thirty-five years ago. It still is something that requires careful reflection and deliberation to answer. Like you, I come from a family where my parents did not finish high school, making it a challenge for me, the first to go to college, to figure whether I could do well (academically) and good (serve my community). I'm here to tell you that the answer is that you can do well and do good. Hill has already talked about some of the successful African-American businessmen, who went from nothing to something. In each case, none were born with silver spoons in their mouths. They all worked hard, resisted temptations, and kept their eyes on the prize. . . . You can do the same. I have gone from being a child of two parents without a high school degree, and who survived on welfare in the 1960s, to becoming an honors graduate, and student body president at Stanford University, and not only a graduate of Harvard Law School, but the seventh African-American, in the history of Harvard Law School, to receive a lifetime appointment as a tenured professor. But understand, from those whom much is given, much is expected. Become the great leader you dream about, but never forget from whence you came. The Village that lifted you up in prayer is still here to celebrate your victories.

Yours in the Struggle,
Professor Charles J. Ogletree, Jr.
Jesse Climenko Professor of Law, and the Founder and Executive Director of the Charles Hamilton Houston Institute for Race and Justice, Harvard Law School

----------Original Message----------

From: Young_Brotha@home.net
Date: August 21, 2005 9:26 PM
To: Hill@manifestyourdestiny.net
Subject: Careers

When you say there are tons of different choices for careers out there for me, what are they? 'Cause I can only think of a couple.

Date: August 22, 2005 9:24 AM
From: Hill@manifestyourdestiny.net
To: Young_Brotha@home.net
Subject: Re: Careers

Man, there are so many different occupations out there for you. I'll give you a partial list in this e-mail for examples, but remember, you can even make up your own career and do something that no one's ever done. There is no limit to what you can do in your life. But here is a real small partial list of occupations:

accountant	fireman	pilot
actor	florist	policeman
airline mechanic	gospel singer	politician
architect	hotel clerk/manager	postal worker
bank teller	investment banker	professional
baseball umpire	IRS employee	athlete
book/magazine editor	jewelry designer	publicist
chef/caterer	landscape designer	real estate agent
chemist	lawyer	restaurant owner
cinematographer	makeup artist	small business owner
computer technician	marine biologist	sports or talent
consultant	minister/preacher	agent
corporate executive	movie director	taxidermist
cosmetologist	movie lighting	teacher
dentist	designer	UPS/FedEx driver
designer	music/film producer	wardrobe stylist
doctor	musician	Web page /graphic
economist	NFL referee	designer
electrician	photographer	writer
film set grip/best boy	physician assistant	zoologist

The best way to think about a career is to ask yourself what it is you love to do, what it is you are good at, and then figure out how to make money doing it. You love video games and are really good at them? Why not have a career creating and designing them, or selling them or marketing them? Make that your goal, and then start working toward it.

Quitting versus
Changing Your Mind

I hated every minute of training, but I said, "Don't quit.
Suffer now and live the rest of your life as a champion."
MUHAMMAD ALI

August 22, 2005
New York

Dear Young Brotha,

Hey man, I'm in New York City shooting *CSI: NY*, and it is
a scorching hot August day. You know what's interesting
about the 22nd of August? It just so happens to be the anniversary date of the largest slave rebellion in U.S. history led
by Nat Turner in 1831—look it up and learn more about it.
Now, that was about 175 years ago; that's a while, isn't it?
America has an incredible history of all types of people fight-
ing for justice, equality, and positive change.

Today I want to talk to you about quitting, because there
are many people in the history of this country who when
faced with adversity never quit; people such as César Chavez,

Martin Luther King, Jr., Muhammad Ali, John F. Kennedy, Rosa Parks, and the above-mentioned Nat Turner. As a matter of fact, anyone who is successful in life, who achieves his goals whether big or small, has done so with perseverance. And at different times *everyone* wants to quit or thinks about quitting, but the winners get past that thought and keep going. Now, I don't need you to lead thousands of people in a revolution. I want you to lead a revolution in your own mind, heart, and spirit. I want you to never quit, even when things get hard or doubt comes into your mind. Lance Armstrong, a gifted athlete who had to quit cycling because of cancer but came back to win the Tour de France (the Super Bowl of bike racing) a record breaking seven times, believes: "Pain is temporary. It may last a minute, or an hour, or a day, or a year, but eventually it will subside and something else will take its place. If I quit, however, it lasts forever."

In your last letter, you said you wanted to "quit" the track team. First of all, I don't like you or anyone in my crew using the word "quit." It is one of those four-letter words that I can't stand. I hate it almost as much as the word "try" (but more on that later). The most important thing for us is to really look at *why* you want to quit something. Before we decide whether you should or should not quit track, we need to analyze it and really know what quitting means. There is a difference between "quitting" something and "changing your mind" and deciding not to do it anymore. I'll explain.

First of all, words have power. By that I mean you could take the exact same action, but if you call it two different things, it will have an effect on the way you approach that action. After Michael Jordan had won numerous championships with the Chicago Bulls, he decided to leave basketball for baseball. After a season on a farm league baseball team, he changed his mind, returned to the Chicago Bulls, and won two more championships. Michael Jordan didn't quit baseball, he changed his mind. He followed his passion to pursue baseball, experienced it, then decided he loved playing in the NBA more. In both cases, he followed his passion; he didn't "quit," he just replaced one passionate pursuit with another.

Words have power.

Let me tell you about my man Steve Jobs, a dude I respect a great deal. He's the guy who created Apple Computers, the iPod, and founded Pixar, the company that makes movies like *Toy Story* and *The Incredibles*. Well, his wealth is so huge he makes Michael Jordan look poor. For the past thirty-three years, every morning Steve Jobs gets up, looks in the mirror, and asks himself, "If today were the last day of my life, would I want to do what I'm about to do today?" If there were a bunch of mornings in a row where the answer was, "No," then he knew he had to change what he was doing. Now, there's nothing wrong with change if you decide to stop doing something that you are not passionate about or that you do not love. There's a poet who I love named Mary Oliver who says, "The only thing you have to do in your life is to let the soft animal of your body love what it loves."

My point is, do what you love so you never have to quit. If you do change what you are doing for the right reasons, then we are not going to call it "quitting," we're going to call it "changing your mind," "doing something else," or "moving on." When you "change what you are doing," that means that you stop doing something that is holding you back from realizing your true destiny. Anything you spend your time doing day in and day out that you are not passionate about is okay to stop doing eventually. (Unless it is school or some other educational experience that is leading you toward a bigger, more passionate goal).

As we discussed, it's important to be active and make decisions and choices. Right? But you can change your mind, and there's nothing wrong with that. Changing your mind is natural. It's okay. It's fine. It's supposed to change. As you learn and experience different things, as you walk through life, you will find you have a new "view" or perspective. This may lead you to want to change your mind. And that's cool.

> Your mind is supposed
> to change.

So given what I just said in this last paragraph, is there anything in your life right now that you want to change your mind about? Maybe you want to join the soccer team instead of the track team, or stop working part time at the fast-food restaurant in order to intern at a law firm, or you might want to pick a new major on your college applications. No, I'm serious; ask yourself that question right now. What in your life do you want to change your mind about? Write it down; then, let's make some changes in that area that you just wrote about, starting today. That's the new version of you, right now. In a week's or day's time, your mind may change about that, and that's cool too. Change is good. Know that!

When you say you are quitting something, it means you're stopping because it's hard, challenging, uncomfortable, or raises some kind of fear in you. If something makes you a little scared, it usually means it's the exact thing you need to complete to go to the next level in your life's journey. Through working hard we develop new skill sets that make us stronger. That's why when someone lifts weights, their muscles become stronger; when you read books, the muscles in your brain become stronger; when speaking in front of a crowd, even though you are afraid, your public speaking muscles become stronger. Let's face it, we are all on life's journey, man, no matter how young or old you are. And the stronger all of our muscles are, the better. Some of us are moving forward, but unfortunately, most people who "quit" things are moving their feet, but getting nowhere or, worse still, moving their feet and going backward. Malcolm X talked about these people: "The treadmill is moving backwards faster than we're able to go forward in this direction. We're not even standing still, we're going backwards." If you quit track only to hang with a group of slackers who have no drive, then you are going backward. But, if you decide you want to give up track in order to spend that time doing something you are passionate about, like playing an instrument or another sport, or even taking a second language, then that is "changing your mind." That is moving forward. Standing still and going backward are no longer options for you and me, so you might as well get comfortable with being successful and unreasonably happy. You're part of my crew now, and all of my crew moves forward in their life's journey. Forward fast. Fast and furious, baby.

I've definitely had my own experiences with "changing my mind" and "doing something else" versus "quitting." After graduating from Harvard Law School, people expected me to slide right into a high-paying job as a lawyer. I even expected to take a job in a law firm because I wanted to pay off my college loans and I knew the job would get me out of debt quickly. But here's what happened: I had already studied and fallen in love with acting. So instead of taking a job in a firm, I moved to Los Angeles and began waiting tables and auditioning for acting jobs. Did I quit law? No, but I changed my mind about law as a career. Was law school a waste of time? Absolutely not. I learned so much and made some of my best friends whom I still have to this day; and, as a matter of fact, I still use my legal skills when I evaluate acting contracts. And since I changed my mind and pursued what I loved, the universe conspired to allow me to pay off my student loans much faster than I ever would have if I had continued to do something I was not passionate about. It works; I am a living testament.

All that said, you asked, should you quit track? No, you shouldn't "quit," but it is okay for you to stop doing it if you clearly aren't passionate about it. I don't think the reason you want to stop running track is because you're afraid. I think the reason you want to end it is because you now know it doesn't fit into your life's journey and it doesn't contribute to your being unreasonably happy. So it's important that when you change your mind, about your A plan, you have a B plan ready. Let's assume running track was your A plan, and since you've changed your mind, you need a B plan. Is there another sport you'd enjoy more? Basketball, hockey, football (my personal favorite), tennis, wrestling, or another I didn't mention? Or do you want to join student government, or the debate team, or the yearbook staff? There are so many other sports and activities that may ignite your passion. The important thing right now is to find the thing you love and do it so that you can be unreasonably happy. So now, it's all about formulating an alternative plan. And that's cool. Feel me?

Man, I gotta get to the set and shoot a scene for *CSI: NY*, so we'll talk soon. E-mail or write me a letter when you can. Peace.

Oh, and I've been writing you from this Chinese restaurant on Broadway, and it's not coincidental that I got a fortune cookie that speaks to exactly what we've been talking about. I'll throw it in the letter, so you can check it out yourself.

Your Friend,

He who has not tasted the bitter does not understand the sweet.

Lucky numbers: 3, 5, 8, 12, 17, 42

Hill

----------Original Message----------

From: Young_Brotha@home.net
Date: August 29, 2005 3:15 PM
To: Hill@manifestyourdestiny.net
Subject: After Graduation

Hill, what if I don't know what I want to do after high school?

Date: August 31, 2005 9:13 AM
From: Hill@manifestyourdestiny.net
To: Young_Brotha@home.net
Subject: Fwd: Re: After Graduation

It would be a miracle if you did know for sure. That's what college is for, a time to explore different possibilities and discover many more options than you could know about in high school. For me, I didn't begin my life's work until I finished *grad* school at the ripe old age of twenty-six. So there is no timetable. Everyone is different. Sooner or later, something will make you excited and joyful just thinking about spending your days doing that, and then you'll know. And guess what? You can choose to do more than one career in a lifetime. But I don't just want you to take my word for it on this one, so I forwarded your question to my boss, Jerry Bruckheimer, one of the most successful television and film producers in history. He is not only responsible for *CSI* and many other TV shows, he has produced all of the *Pirates of the Caribbean* movies, *Pearl Harbor, The Rock, Remember the Titans, Bad Boys I* and *II*, and all of the *Beverly Hills Cop* movies (just to name a few). Now, I didn't tell him what I said, I just asked him to answer the question for you. Look at how similar his answer is to mine.

HH

---------Begin Forwarded Message----------

I wouldn't worry too much if you aren't sure what to do by the time you graduate high school. College is really the place where you begin not only the journey through academics to hone your interests, but also where you embark on self discovery. College made me aware of professional opportunities that I hadn't previously considered. But further—and even more essential—it provided an environment that fostered personal growth.

After college, I landed my first job in the mailroom of an advertising agency. From there, as I took on new jobs and challenges, I consistently drew on the experiences, tools, and education gained in college. My college years helped prepare me for my career as a motion picture producer.

Jerry Bruckheimer

----------Reply Message----------

>>Thanks, Jerry. I'll pass this on to him.
>>
>>HH

---------Original Message----------

From: Young_Brotha@home.net
Date: September 2, 2005 8:39 PM
To: Hill@manifestyourdestiny.net
Subject: School

Hill, what if school is not for me?

Date: September 3, 2005 2:32 PM
From: Hill@manifestyourdestiny.net
To: Young_Brotha@home.net
Subject: Re: School

Where did you get the idea that school is not for you? Come on. Wake up and look around. We live in an information age, and initially school is the best place to learn where to find the information that is best for you and your life. Life is a journey, and everything in life is done in its proper time. And young people need school for experience and information. Like I've told you before: Use school. Don't let school use you.

But there are some people that traditional school may not be the best situation for, for a whole list of reasons. Like they might have dyslexia, Attention Deficit Disorder, malnutrition, need glasses, or just have extremely poor teachers or a horrible teaching environment, like other students who harass them. School is still for them, it just may not be the school that they are in. If one of those is the case for you and you're just not telling me, then we need to find you a new school.

HH

Tools of Choice: Educating and Money-Making

Knowledge is the best weapon to combat any war right now. Everything is moving toward being a mental war, you have to feed your mind and stockpile your ammo for this mental war. School is the start.

DAVID BANNER

September 15, 2005
Chicago

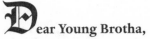ear Young Brotha,

I just finished reading your last letter. You said you wanted to talk about money and how you are frustrated you don't have any right now. But before we talk about money, I want to give you some props. You must have clearly understood me in my last letter saying, "Words have power." So don't think I didn't notice that you said, "I don't have any money *right now*" as opposed to just saying, "I don't have any money." Your use of the words "right now" shows that you see this as a temporary condition, and you are choosing your language to reflect that. Excellent, my brotha. Now, let's talk about money.

No doubt, money is one of the most powerful tools available in this lifetime. But that's all it is: a "tool." It is a tool that gives you choices. How does education relate to that? Education is just like money. It is a tool that also buys you choices. On a real level, education and money are the same currency in the world. They're both tools that buy and afford you choices. Do you see how money and education relate? The more you learn, the more valuable you become and the more you can maneuver in the world, whether it's jobs, travel, or connections. It's the same with money.

There is no doubt that money plays a huge role in each and every one of our lives on a daily basis. So much so that when asked the question, "What do you want most in your life?" most people answer, "Lots of money." The need and want for money is consuming. People don't usually say, "I want to be unreasonably happy." They don't say, "I want my family to be unreasonably happy," nor do they say, "I want to be healthy and happy." They usually turn first to their desire for money. Check it out, there's nothing wrong with wanting money. I want money. Me, Hill Harper. I like money. But, I also realize that the old saying, "There are some things that money can't buy," is true. In fact, if you break it down, money can buy one thing, and one thing only, and you know what that is? Options. Money is great because it can buy you options. Money cannot buy you freedom or happiness or love. If you have enough money, it gives you options as to what you can do in your life and with your life. If you have enough money, you can go anywhere you want or buy whatever you want. Every "option" is on the table. If you have enough money and you get sick, you can afford to go to any hospital you want. See, that's where money ends, with options. If you are sick and dying, money can't make you well.

All money can buy you is options, and that's pretty good. The more options we have, the more ability we have to change directions on the journey to being unreasonably happy.

So where does hope fit in? In today's world, education, technology,

> *All that money can buy you is options.*

and money all buy options. That's why they are linked to hope. For instance, since money can only buy you options, options have a direct effect on hope. Because if you have many options at your disposal, it's much easier to be "hope-full." If one option sucks, then you have other options that probably won't suck. That's one way money and hope are related.

Most people who are struggling with money issues, or a basic lack of money, obsess about it day and night, believing that if they can just get more it will magically solve all their problems and make them happy. Money will solve your financial problems, but money has never made anybody happy. If you aren't happy now, believe me, money will not change that. People spend their lives chasing dreams they hope will make them rich. They even try to shortcut the process by making "easy" money by breaking the law: stealing, scamming, dealing drugs. All of these illegal ways to make "easy money" carry the risk of "hard time"—jail. There is no such thing as "easy money."

Money, however it comes to you, is not the root cause of happiness. Nothing tangible and outside of yourself can ever be the source of your happiness. It is important then to ask yourself: What qualities do I need to embody in order to be happy? For me, it is the loving relationships I have with my friends and family, my work as an actor and artist, and my newfound exchange of letters with you. Those things make me happy. More focus needs to be put on developing an inner happiness, doing what you love, and having faith that if you do these things, the money will come. Imagine having all the money you could ever need and the next day it is gone, like in the stock market crash in the 1920s. People were jumping out of buildings and off of bridges. People lost all of their money and then they lost their minds all because of their unhealthy attachment to money. Liking money is healthy. Putting the desire for money above your desire for health and happiness is unhealthy. I promise you, work on being happy, find the thing you love to do; pursue that, and the money will follow.

Your generation is in the toughest position in recent history. It's no wonder that many of you have little hope for your future and don't think you'll ever be able to buy a piece of real estate or get out of debt or succeed. Your generation is the first one that will never know what it means to have job security. The days of people staying in a job for thirty years are, for the most part, over. It's not surprising so many in your generation are seriously depressed about their future, and with no hope many of you have given up. You've decided that you're not only broken financially, but your spirit is broken as well. Well, that's what many think, but here's the deal.

It would appear that most young people are "broke" by circumstance, right? One, the cost of educating yourself and student loan debt is huge. And two, the job market is shrinking because our country is exporting many of our jobs overseas where the cost of living is much lower and, therefore, the companies pay the workers much less. What does that mean? It means that you've been born into a generation where the cost of everything is higher, but your ability to make money, i.e., buy options, is lower. You don't know what to do because no one is teaching you how to navigate in this new landscape. Your parents and your grandparents don't know how to teach you because they grew up in a different time with different circumstances where everything was expanding, not contracting. Your school's curriculum, which means what they're trying to teach you, is probably out-of-date for today's reality as well.

Music seems to be one of the only areas where lessons seem to be handed down in this new way of the world. However, the new lessons in music aren't necessarily the ones that may serve you best either. For instance, a few years ago there was this rap song by The Lox w/Lil' Kim called "Money, Power & Respect" and one of the lines went, "First you get the money, then you get the power . . ." In the song they were presenting wrong information in the wrong order. A more accurate way of breaking it down would be a song titled, "Power, Respect, Money." First you get the power by getting a good education and setting yourself up for success at whatever you do. Education, clear and simple, is power. Then you get the respect, because by committing yourself to learning and strengthening your mind, you gain self-respect and the respect of all those friends and family members around you. And last but not least, you get the money, because the more education you have, the higher salary you can command in the job market.

On the face of it, everything seems to be going against your generation. But, that's not true. Why? Because your generation has more choices and opportunities than any generation before it. Like I said earlier, money is simply a tool to give you choices. As are technology and your ability to communicate and connect with more people than any generation in the history of the world. Use all of these tools. One surefire way to bring more money and opportunities into our lives is to integrate technology with education. This will give you more job options, jobs with higher salaries, and because your generation is more technology savvy, the playing field (in terms of education and jobs) has been leveled more so than it ever was in the past. There are jobs today that weren't even created when I first entered the job market, such as a Web-page designer or an eBay specialist. I have a friend who paid off twenty thousand dollars in six months for a baby grand piano by selling her old clothing on eBay. That is what I call a modern day supercharged yard sale. To have access to a great deal of information quickly and cheaply is like having your own private think tank of information. And it's up to you how you choose to use all of that information. You can also research things that you might be interested in. This new information-driven world is completely structured around choices, and your success is completely dependent on you making the right ones. And the "right choice" has everything to do with you following your heart, passion, and those things for which you are "hope-full."

> Money is simply a tool
> to give you choices.

Having more choices greatly increases your chances of success. When I was doing the basketball movie *He Got Game*, I got a chance to play ball with my costar and NBA all-star Ray Allen. He said to me that even though he is right-handed, he has for many years worked very hard to develop his left hand to be equal to his right. He said that sometimes a defender will cut off the right side of the court, and since he's developed his left, he now has the *choice* to go left and score.

If he hadn't developed his left hand, his only choice would be to go right, greatly decreasing his chance of scoring. He made sure that he became the best possible player he could be in order to increase his chance for success. Having tools that give us choices like education, information technology, and resources (money) increases our chance of (but doesn't guarantee) success. Not even Ray Allen makes every shot. But that doesn't mean he stops shooting.

All right man, I gotta jump on this plane and get back to L.A. I love Chi-town: incredible pizza and great blues. You like the blues? Oh man, it's a great style of music. It's like slow rock and rap smashed together. Check out John Lee Hooker sometime, or B.B. King. You talk about *passion*. Oh Baby. They are *hot*!

I'm boarding the plane. Hit me back via that computer you are so good at. Talk to you soon.

Your Friend,

Hill

----------Original Message----------

From: Young_Brotha@home.net
Date: September 30, 2005 11:22 AM
To: Hill@manifestyourdestiny.net
Subject: Salary

Hill, what is a good salary to make?

Date: October 1, 2005 12:48 PM
From: Hill@manifestyourdestiny.net
To: Young_Brotha@home.net
Subject: Re: Salary

A "good salary" is an income that covers your living expenses plus
regular savings. By living expenses I mean rent or mortgage, food,
utilities, and transportation to work (etc.). Different people have
different "living expenses" because cost of living varies from place
to place.

I'll show you what I mean. First of all, your monthly expenses
should never exceed your monthly income. Say you're working a
job that pays you thirteen dollars an hour and you work forty hours
a week. Your yearly salary would be $24,960 dollars a year. That
breaks down to $520 dollars a week and $2,080 a month. Keep in
mind that your rent or mortgage payment should not be more than
25 percent of your monthly salary. So that leaves you with three
weeks pay for food, utilities, car insurance, entertainment, and savings. It is a good habit to deposit 10 percent of your weekly salary
into a savings account and pretend it doesn't exist. That money will
grow over time and become your wealth base. (In addition to a
savings account you could put your money in what is called a "mu-
tual fund"—they operate out of the stock market and can be set
up to get automatic deposits and can act like a savings account—

an example of one is Vanguard 500). Notice in the chart below I have no line for credit card expenses because remember the "Debt Rule," we do not believe in having any credit card debt. Here's a sample of monthly expenses:

Monthly income: $2,080
Rent or mortgage: $520
Utilities & cable: $200
Phones: $80
Car insurance & gas: $120
Food & groceries: $300

Clothing: $120
Entertainment (music, movies, games): $150
IRS & state taxes: $250
Savings: $200
Church or charitable donations: $100

With the above salary and expenses, that leaves only about $40 at the end of each month, but that is fine because you've covered everything you need to use money for. So you keep that $40 in your bank account as "just in case" money. If you want to learn more about managing your money, you can check out these two books: *The Money Book for the Young, Fabulous & Broke* by Suze Orman and *Wealth Happens One Day at a Time* by Brooke M. Stephens.

HH

----------Original Message----------

From: Young_Brotha@home.net
Date: October 3, 2005 8:34 PM
To: Hill@manifestyourdestiny.net
Subject: Cars

Okay, so in your last e-mail, you've got me spending $120 a month on gas and insurance for a car, but I don't have one yet. What do I need to actually buy a car?

Date: October 4, 2005 9:29 AM
From: Hill@manifestyourdestiny.net
To: Young_Brotha@home.net
Subject: Re: Cars

Some people would say good credit and a loan, but as you know from my letter to you talking about the "Debt Rule," I'm not one of those people. What you need to buy a car is the cash to pay for that car and to be able to afford the monthly insurance, gas, and maintenance fees. If you don't have a lot of money, there are a lot of very reliable used cars that are not very expensive. The first car I bought was a thirteen-year-old green Toyota Corolla station wagon that was a little rusty around the door edges. My friends jokingly called it "The Green Hornet." The Green Hornet had 167,000 miles on it, and cost me $500. I paid cash, and I wasn't embarrassed driving it because I paid for it with my own money. And it did the job a car was supposed to do. It got me from point A to point B safely and reliably. When you buy a used car make sure you don't spend more than it's worth—check out the values of different makes and years on the Blue Book Web site (www.kbb.com). And have a mechanic look at it before handing over your money so you don't get a lemon.

HH

Part Three

The Real Deal:
Girls, Sex, and
Responsibility

MANifest Your Destiny

Finding Your Swagga

*Cool is not just one type of cool. Cool is confidence and knowing.
Some people can be what people call "nerds" and they're cool because they
know what they are that makes them cool, and somebody
aspires to be like them, because they're fine with it.
It's confidence.*

ANDRE 3000

October 16, 2005
Miami

Dear Young Brotha,

In your last letter, you mostly asked questions about girls. You said you assumed I don't have any problems meeting girls since *People* magazine named me one of the sexiest men alive last year. Don't be fooled; you and I are in the same boat when it comes to girls. Whether you're in a magazine or not, it's not easy to meet and connect with girls. I guess that subject is dominating your mind right now, which is normal. It seems that this girl named Jamilla keeps coming up. You like her? You can tell me, it's cool. It's great to have a crush. I have one right now too. You know how it makes your heart beat a little faster? I keep thinking about her, and sometimes my mind will just wander to her and it will make me smile. Does that happen to you? I'm in Miami, getting ready to go to the MTV Video Music Awards tonight; it's gonna be mad fun. And better yet, the girl I have a crush on is down here too.

So you ended your letter asking, "How do I get girls?" That's a very good question, and I'm going to answer it right now. Listen closely. The key to getting girls is to simply . . . find "your swagga."

You ever notice how the greatest men seem to have a confident swagger? Think about Muhammad Ali, Michael Jordan, Jay-Z, Tiger Woods, or even Donald Trump. Their swagger comes from them living their truth. Now what do I mean by "living their truth?" Living your truth means behaving as the most truthful representation of who you are. If you are completely yourself, you will exhibit your own unique "swagger." You will reveal your own style or mojo. It will not copy anybody else's style. It's like a rap flow. 50 and Mos Def are both rappers from New York, but their sound is completely different. Then you have East Coast, West Coast, and rappers from the Dirty Dirty, but they all are unique and have their own individual flow. You see what I'm saying? When you are truly yourself that means you are living fearlessly, and a truly fearless man is very attractive to girls. Now I'm not talking about false bravado or false confidence, like the dudes who run around saying, "I don't give a f***." That's not truth, that's them trying to convince you and themselves of their truth, but they're really just lying, like the peacock that pokes out his chest at a predator hoping that the plumes of feathers will make him seem tougher than he really is. Any girl worth dating can see through that false bravado and is attracted to a man who is living his truth.

Why is living your truth so effective in helping you get girls? Well, your truth is a completely unique and special representation of you in the world, and girls are attracted to that. Your truth is different from any other person's truth. That's why it's so amazing to be human. We all want something special and unique. The ability to be yourself, to stay in the game and to work smart makes you a success. Nothing is more attractive to a woman than a man who is his

Women love originals.

real self. What girl wouldn't rather have an original Prada purse than a knockoff? Women love originals. Check out Lenny Kravitz or David Beckham. They are girl magnets, and they are truly original. Be your authentic self first and foremost. Some girls might be caught up in the glare of a guy with bling-bling, but that's a smoke screen, and over time it fades. Your job is to be a real diamond that becomes brighter and more valuable over time.

Girls are attracted to true confidence. Your true sense of self is represented by strong humility, kindness, and the desire to do the right thing, but at the very same time having the spirit of a warrior. And what I mean by "spirit of a warrior" is a man who takes actions with a level of energy that matches that of a warrior going to battle. This level of energy is represented by people who are truly active and passionate in the actions they take, like Lance Armstrong riding in the Tour de France or how the best teacher in your school teaches her class. The spirit of a warrior is the opposite of the peacock poking out his chest and showing his feathers. When you combine honesty, kindness, and humility with a warrior's spirit, some people call that being a

"Peaceful Warrior." Take it from me Young Brotha, Peaceful Warriors get girls!

The crazy part about living like a Peaceful Warrior is that I don't live that way to get girls. It's just an extra added bonus. I think the reason I have had the pleasure of dating some of the most beautiful, successful, and intelligent women in the world is because I live with passion in my heart and compassion in my spirit. I live that way because it's the true reflection of who I am. The one great benefit of living my truth and having the swagger that comes with that truth is that a lot of girls are attracted to me simply because I'm being my authentic self. You can live your dynamic, passionate, creative, "Peaceful Warrior" truth as well. When you live your truth, you can't help but have a humble swagger.

Call that girl Jamilla, introduce yourself in a Peaceful Warrior style—in the style of a guy who is energetically living from his truth. Ask her out to the mall or somewhere fun in a very humble and confident way. First, take a few deep breaths, center yourself, and remember you are happy and you are authentic. Be yourself, the self that has no substitute.

All right, man. Do it! Okay. I've got to run to the VMAs. Let me know how it turns out with Jamilla. Much love and blessings.

Your Peaceful Warrior Friend,

Hill

My grandfather Hill in 1931, age twenty-four, when he graduated from Meharry Medical College School of Pharmacy in Nashville, Tennessee

My grandfather Hill at age twenty-nine in front of Piedmont Pharmacy (Seneca, South Carolina), which he owned and personally worked in every day from 1936 to 1991

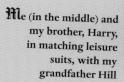

Me (in the middle) and my brother, Harry, in matching leisure suits, with my grandfather Hill

My grandfather Harper,
at his farm in Iowa

Me (age two) and my brother (age five) with my grandfather
Harper

Me with my mom and dad at a party in Boston after my graduation from Harvard. Although they had been divorced for years, it was so important that they could still be supportive of me even though they were no longer together.

Cheesing it up at my graduation from Harvard Law School and the Kennedy School of Government

Me across the street from the Empire State Building with the cast of CSI: NY. *From left to right*: Gary Sinise, Eddie Cahill, Melina Kanakaredes, and me

On location scuba diving on the set of *CSI: NY*. In this scene, I had to recover a body that was dumped in the water.

A shot of me filming on the set of *CSI: NY*. I'm examining a dead body, looking for evidence that might give clues as to how she died or who might have hurt her. And what's amazing is that the woman is really a live actress—it's not a dummy. The makeup artists on my show are incredibly talented.

𝔐e and Quincy Jones at the 2005 Black Movie Awards. I was there because a film I did, *Lackawanna Blues,* was nominated for an award. Standing next to someone like Mr. Jones, you can feel the genius and greatness beside you.

𝔐e with Regina King *(left)* and Vivica Fox *(right),* at the 2005 Black Movie Awards. Sandwiched between two of the most beautiful women in Hollywood . . . life is good.

𝕸e and Halle Berry at the *Entertainment Weekly* party, the night before the 2005 Emmy Awards

𝕸e and Jay-Z, after seeing a play at the Ivar Theater in L.A.

JEFF VESPA

Me and pro skater Tony Hawk, at a 2005 MTV Video Music Awards pre-party in Miami. I wonder if I could hit him up for some skating lessons . . . .

Clowning with Chris Rock at Jamie Foxx's birthday blowout in Beverly Hills

Catching up with rapper The Game, also at Jamie's birthday

𝔐e and Venus Williams at Koi restaurant in L.A.

𝔐e and Ludacris, "rollin' out," at a 2005 BET Music Awards after-party in L.A.

𝔐e with Nick Cannon and Gabrielle Union, at Diddy's 2005 pre-VMA dinner at the Setai Hotel in Miami

----------Original Message----------

From: Young_Brotha@home.net
Date: October 25, 2005 3:44 PM
To: Hill@manifestyourdestiny.net
Subject: What Women Want

Hill, are women only interested in men with hot cars, money, and muscle?

Date: October 26, 2005 9:23 AM
From: Hill@manifestyourdestiny.net
To: Young_Brotha@home.net
Subject: Re: What Women Want

Women care about much more than just external things. A woman wants a man who will treat her with respect and wants to do fun things with her and make her laugh. Case in point: One of my cars is a Toyota Prius (one of the slowest cars on the road) and I'm only 160 lbs soaking wet and still I get lots of girls. A good joke, kindness, and a giving spirit will go a lot further than muscles, money, and hot cars. And remember, the brain is a muscle too!

But I definitely don't want you to just take my word on this one. So I forwarded your question to my friend Sanaa Lathan. I have known Sanaa for over ten years, long before either of us had starred in movies, and she is one of the most intelligent, beautiful, and talented women I know. She got her graduate degree from Yale University and then broke out when she starred in *Love and Basketball*. Did you see it? She has since starred in a movie I know you saw, *AVP: Alien vs. Predator*. I didn't tell her what I wrote to you and look how similar to my answer her reply to your question is. Sanaa wrote:

----------Begin Forwarded Message----------

Absolutely not! All I want to know is can I talk to him? Is he really interested in getting to know how my mind works? Does he truly listen when we talk? Do we have fun, do we laugh, and ultimately how do I feel when we're together? Be careful of wearing too much bling cuz it might outshine your better qualities. Xo Sanaa

----------Original Message----------

From: Young_Brotha@home.net
Date: October 29, 2005 10:22 PM
To: Hill@manifestyourdestiny.net
Subject: Girl(s)

Hill, what's wrong with seeing more than one girl?

Date: October 30, 2005 11:03 AM
From: Hill@manifestyourdestiny.net
To: Young_Brotha@home.net
Subject: Re: Girl(s)

Hey man, the issue here is honesty versus deception. If you are clear and straight with each girl and not deceiving anyone, there is nothing wrong with dating more than one person. Unfortunately, a lot of dudes are not always honest. Many guys I know try to justify their deception by saying they "have to lie." That's BS.

Just know going in that the prevailing social pattern in our culture is a one-on-one relationship. Many girls may not be down for you seeing others. So, if you are dating more than one girl, and you say to each that she is the only one you're seeing, that is very wrong because it's dishonest. It's a lie. So it doesn't matter if you choose to date more than one woman or just one, what matters is that you be honest with everyone that you date, all the time.

HH

Sex Matters

Love does not begin and end the way we seem to think it does.
Love is a battle; love is a war; love is a growing up.
JAMES BALDWIN

November 1, 2005
Los Angeles

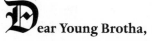ear Young Brotha,

In your letter you asked me about sex. Not the easiest or simplest subject to address, but it's something we should definitely talk about. But I must say this, you are moving pretty fast from barely being able to ask Jamilla to the mall less than a month ago, and now talking about having sex. Dang.

There are so many important issues involving sex that it can easily be very confusing. So I'm glad you wrote and asked me my advice "brother to brother."

Physically speaking, sex is not difficult. Millions of people around the world "do it." Everywhere you look something alludes to sex as if sex is always easy to get and always fun to have. Sex sells. It sells music when you see a video of half-naked women fawning over a male singer, it sells sneakers when you see cheerleaders in short-shorts cheering for Iverson, or the car advertisement when you see the cute girl riding in the passenger seat of some car they are selling. Sex sells beer, cigarettes, burgers, and movies. The fastest growing sector of the magazine industry is comprised of publications like *Maxim, Stuff,* and *FHM.* Advertisers tout casual sex as the new cool. But fantasy sex with the latest *Maxim* cover girl is not what you and I have to talk about. We need to discuss the real deal: You, your "private parts," and what you *choose* to do with them.

When you are young and you really feel like you want to have sex—right now—it is partially because your hormones, which are chemicals in your body, can be out of balance. At different times during adolescence your body may have too much of some hormones and not enough of others, which can cause your emotions to be out of whack. These hormones help you mature into being an adult and take you from being a boy to becoming a man. They eventually normalize and smooth out. Until then though, off-kilter hormones can overpower you and overwhelm your judgment. And bad judgment and sex are a dangerous combination. "A recipe for disaster" as my friend Donovan McNabb would say. And we don't want disasters.

So let me get this straight, in your letter you said you wanted to talk about sex, but the specific story you're telling me is about you and Jamilla. You said you've been dating Jamilla, and she doesn't want to have sex at this point in your relationship. You say you're ready to take the relationship to the next level, and if she really trusts you, she will too. Then there's this other girl, Crystal, who you say wants to get with you right now and isn't trippin' about having sex. First of all, there are a whole lot of issues besides sex in your scenario. Principally, there are the issues of your honesty, fidelity, and the agreements that you have made with Jamilla in being her "boyfriend." If dating another woman is something you're interested in, that is something that you need to be clear about with

> *Bad judgment and sex are a dangerous combination.*

Jamilla. That has nothing to do with "sex" per se. It has everything to do with you making decisions that will affect your friendship and relationship with Jamilla.

One thing I would like you to consider is the misconception that the more sexual conquests you have, the more masculine you are. The number of sexual conquests has nothing to do with a man's masculinity. It is often the case that men try to hide their insecurities by sleeping with multiple women. But there is more value in developing a long-term relationship; you have a best friend who knows you well, you have someone you trust, and you feel valuable in a relationship. If you choose to break up with Jamilla and pursue a relationship with Crystal, you have to realize that you run the risk of never getting back to the same place with Jamilla. So, you have to decide if your relationship with Jamilla is worth risking. But since you didn't ask about all that, and you specifically asked about sex, then that's what we'll talk about.

Okay, I'm about to make a big statement right now, and I want you to get this clearly. Here it is, and you can quote me on this: Throughout the history of the world more men have been brought down and had their lives destroyed because of their irresponsible sexual activity than by any other single act. That's right. Wow. Did you get that? But the key to understanding that fact is to really break down what I mean when I say "irresponsible sexual activity." Notice I didn't just say "sexual activity" like a lot of people would say to you, as if they are trying to make you think that sex itself is a bad thing. Sex is not a bad thing. That is because the act of having sexual relations is the most natural thing in the world. Sex is a blessing given to us by God for all of us to derive pleasure from and to procreate and keep the human species going. God made it feel good so we would be encouraged to keep doing it more and more. But with that blessing comes a huge responsibility. What commonly happens all over the world with boys and men is that we let the feeling or idea of sex cloud our judgment and often we make irresponsible choices and take irresponsible actions. That's what I mean when I say "irresponsible sexual activity."

Irresponsible sexual activity is any sexual activity that is engaged in without both parties being fully and completely responsible about how they approach sex. Having sex is a big deal. It is one of the most fundamentally personal and intimate relations you can have with someone, not to mention the fact that there are numerous potentially negative consequences that can come out of any single sexual experience.

God and this universe are structured such that if we make responsible choices in anything we do, we will tend to receive a blessing from that choice. Responsible choices in sex are no different. Sex is supposed to feel good and that is why if you are ever having sex, or contemplating having sex, and it doesn't seem completely right for both of you, then you should not be having sex.

For instance, even if you weren't dating Jamilla, do you

think it would be a responsible choice for you to have sex with Crystal? If both you and Crystal decided to have sex, have you considered all of the components and issues that come with having sex with her? In other words, have you or would you discuss sexually transmitted diseases with her? Would you both get tested for STDs before you engaged in sex? Have you or would you talk about protection—using condoms? And that means using condoms whether she is taking birth control or not, because condoms are about more than just not getting someone pregnant. Condoms are about protecting the health and safety of you and your partner. These are not negotiable points. They are essential for responsible sexual activity.

Clearly, I think the best choice is for you to stay with Jamilla because you care about each other. You do not need to rush into having sex at this point in your life. There are a whole lot of steps and a number of conversations you need to have if you decide you want to entertain dating Crystal. Ask yourself, are you interested in dating her because you like her, or is it the easy sex? And remember, just because a woman wants to have sex with you, it doesn't mean you should feel you have to have sex with her. I was nineteen years old and a sophomore in college when I lost my virginity. During high school there were numerous times that I could have had sex, but I chose not to, because I wasn't ready. I wasn't ready to have sex responsibly then, but as you'll see when we discuss mistakes, no matter how old you are, you can still make mistakes in the area of sex. I've made them, and you will probably make them, but we can be courageous and attempt to minimize mistakes. Like I said above, sex is a big deal, and irresponsible sexual activity has ruined many, many lives because of the consequences of both sexually transmitted diseases and negative choices in choosing partners. Men have lost their jobs, committed crimes of passion, and been sent to their death; families have been torn apart by extramarital affairs; the respect of friends and good standing in the community have been sacrificed because of irresponsible sexual activity.

Having sex with a woman doesn't make you more of a man. Unless you're having sex for all of the right reasons, you're actually less manly and more boyish for feeling like you need to have irresponsible sex. No matter what choices you make, I will be here for you, but I would be very disappointed if you choose to be irresponsible in the area of sex. This is your future you're gambling with.

> *This is your future*
> *you're gambling with.*

I remember when I was your age. Just like you, there were some days I couldn't stop thinking about sex. As I said earlier, your strong urges to have sex are from hormones—that's why there are some times when you are more hyped-up about having sex than others. Some people call that feeling "horny," which in and of itself is kind of a funny word, but the word "horny" comes out of the word "hormones." That feeling of wanting to have sex right now is the direct result of chemicals in your body. I'll tell you an embarrassing story; at least it felt embarrassing for me at the time. In high school, I was visiting my mom and she thought I was going to have sex with this hot girl named Regina. She was so worried that I would get Regina pregnant and ruin my future that she decided she needed to have a talk with me. One night, my mother pulled me aside before I was going out and said, "Hill, I know your body feels like it needs to have sex, but I don't want you to be having sex with Regina. Can't you just masturbate more?" And I was like, "Mom, I can't believe you just said that to me." I was embarrassed at the time, but looking back, I think it was great that my mom was able to talk with me about sex. Most parents don't talk about sex until it's too late. That is why I am so proud of you for writing to me and opening up a discussion about sex. A lot of people consider sex a taboo subject, but it is essential that you discuss it with people you trust. Above all, always discuss all aspects of sex with anyone you may choose to be intimate with.

I know this letter is going to lead to more questions so write me back or e-mail me when you can. I'll always answer.

Okay, I've gotta go shoot this love scene for this movie I'm working on. Which reminds me, sex and love scenes in movies aren't real; they're even filmed in front of a huge crew of people. I think that because of movies, a lot of people have overglamorized notions of what sex is and how it should be. Don't be fooled. Real sex in real life comes with real consequences.

Hit me back. Until then, be well.

Your Friend,

Hill

----------Original Message----------

From: Young_Brotha@home.net
Date: November 4, 2005 10:55 PM
To: Hill@manifestyourdestiny.net
Subject: Girl Complications

Hill,

Why do girls change their minds a lot and act so complicated?

Date: November 6, 2005 3:10 PM
From: Hill@manifestyourdestiny.net
To: Young_Brotha@home.net
Subject: Fwd: Re: Girl Complications

That is a great question—one that I think can best be answered by one of the smartest and prettiest women I know—Gabrielle Union. She is one of my best friends and a great actress—she played Eva in *Deliver Us from Eva* with LL Cool J, and she was the cool sexy cop and Will Smith's girlfriend in *Bad Boys II*. Remember the head cheerleader for the Compton Clovers in *Bring It On*? That's her. She and I did the TV show *City of Angels* together. Anyway, I'm going to forward this question to her and ask her to answer it for you.

HH

----------Begin Forwarded Message----------

Oftentimes as girls and young women, we can be insecure and not always confident enough to say exactly what we really mean. Since we are maturing, we are constantly evolving and what we like and don't like is continually changing. Part of it is that we are all on a journey of self-discovery and someone or something that may seem exciting one day doesn't interest us the next. The same is true for boys and young men. Part of maturing is figuring out what works for you, and the same holds true for girls. So we need to cut each other some slack. But here is a secret: If you want to know how you can best understand the "complicated" actions of a girl, the best thing to do is to listen to what she is saying, and if she seems to contradict herself a lot or act "complicated" then just calmly ask her questions. By asking questions and communicating clearly it will help both of you understand what each of you wants and if you are right for each other. Remember a lot of girls think boys are complicated too. Communication and questions can help cut down on the "complications."

Best Wishes, Gabrielle Union

Mistakes

If you live long enough, you'll make mistakes.
But if you learn from them, you'll be a better person.
It's how you handle adversity, not how it affects you.
BILL CLINTON

November 12, 2005
Los Angeles

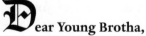ear Young Brotha,

I knew my letter to you about sex would elicit a whole lot of questions. However, I didn't anticipate that you wouldn't follow my advice. So, if I understood your letter correctly, you and Jamilla decided to break up and you decided to start dating Crystal. After dating Crystal, you decided you wanted to have sex. And from the way you described how it went down, the sex you decided to have was what I called "irresponsible sex," meaning you didn't have all the conversations or make the choices that would lead to protecting yourself and Crystal. In your letter, you say you got caught up in the moment, and you didn't have any condoms, and—even if you would have thought of them—you didn't have any money to buy them. My first question is, if you didn't have money for condoms, do you have money to raise a baby? Children are expensive and forever.

You say that you made a mistake and that you are disappointed in yourself. Well, I'm not gonna lie. I'm disappointed in you too. That doesn't mean I love you any less, but I am still disappointed. I just want what's best for you. This might sound harsh but, no one put a gun to your head and said, "You have to have sex. Right here, right now." If that was not the right time, meaning you didn't have protection and you hadn't had the proper discussions with your partner to make sure that this was a completely positive thing for both of you, then you did make a mistake. Keeping it real, you chose to be irresponsible, and there's no excuse because you had all the information you needed on how not to make a mistake.

But that being the case, know this: Mistakes are a part of every person's life.

We all make mistakes.

You will make more mistakes over the course of your life, as will I. All of us make mistakes in many areas of our lives, not just sexually. But, the bad thing about mistakes in the sexual context is that some of those mistakes can affect us for the rest of our lives. Mistakes happen very quickly, often when we are distracted and not paying close attention, and like I said, we all make them. It doesn't matter how old or young you are, you can still make mistakes, whether it's your first time having sex or not. Each time you embark on a sexual relationship, new or continued, there's potential for mak-

> *We all make mistakes.*

ing a mistake. I'm not going to sit here and act like I've never made a mistake in the area of sex. It can happen very easily, but that is no excuse. For instance, the second time I ever had sex, I made a huge mistake.

I met this girl one summer break during college, and we were feeling each other. One day she came to visit me at my mom's house, and we were so into each other that the second she walked in the door, it seemed like we were kissing and clothes were flying off. I was definitely caught up in the moment and, like you, I was not taking my time to make responsible choices. I was so excited by the opportunity that I wasn't thinking clearly. So, as you can probably guess, she wanted to have sex, and so did I. Rather than discuss the issues of sex and protection, rather than risk the mood with an awkward conversation, I chose to be irresponsible, and I made a big mistake. I didn't have any condoms, and she said that she couldn't get pregnant because she had just come off her period, which, by the way, was a mistake on her part— each woman is different but I've heard of women getting pregnant while still having their period, so don't think that's birth control—you never know. Being caught up in the moment, hormones raging, we didn't discuss it any further; I remember much less about the actual sex than I remember what resulted from it. As I've said to you before, all of us make mistakes, and having unprotected sex that day was my big mistake. I was in *college* at the time, and I was supposed to be smarter than that. But I wasn't.

So what do you think happened? Did she get pregnant? She could have, easily. We didn't use protection, or any type of birth control: huge mistake. But luckily, she didn't. Did she contract an STD from me? She could have, but luckily, she didn't. Did I contract an STD from her? Yes, I did. About a week later, I started having shooting pain every time I urinated. I dreaded going to the bathroom because it burned so bad. Terrified for my life and my future ability to have children, I went alone to the doctor. I was working a summer job so I scheduled the doctor's appointment during my lunch break. The doctor tested me and learned that I had contracted chlamydia, which, like all sexually transmitted diseases, is dangerous and very easily transmitted. Like most sexually transmitted diseases you cannot tell someone is infected "just by looking at them." Normal girls, and guys for that matter, can and do get sexually transmitted diseases. After all, I think of myself as a normal guy, yet, here I was caught out there with an STD. This was only my second time ever having sex, but I still got an STD. I was not only embarrassed, I was disappointed in myself, and I told no one about it. I was very lucky. Chlamydia is one of the STDs that is easily curable (for men, at least), but if I hadn't gone to the doctor I could have become sterile—or spread it to someone else. The doctor gave me a prescription, and very quickly I was cured and healthy. But just the fact that medicine was able to cure me doesn't make my mistake any less dangerous. I could have easily contracted one of the STDs that is not curable, like herpes, and I would have had to live with it for the rest of my life, or it could have potentially killed me, like HIV. I could have gotten a young woman that I was not married to pregnant. I could have had a "baby-mama" who I knew little about and there we were, risking bringing an unwanted child into the world. We were both at a time in our lives when neither of us would have been ready to be responsible parents. God was looking out for us. I was lucky, but I don't want you to contract an STD or get someone pregnant to learn a lesson. You can be smarter than I and not make the same mistakes I've made. I will tell you this: I have never ever made this mistake again. While accidents and mistakes can and do happen, the most important thing is to learn from them so that we don't have to make them more than once. And mistakes can happen no matter how young or old you are.

Hopefully, by sharing this story with you, you'll think about the choices you make and how you approach any sexual activity, whether it is with Crystal or any other woman you meet over the course of your life. Young or old, it is our responsibility as men to make responsible choices with regard to sex. No matter what a woman says, if you choose to have sex with her, as a man it is your responsibility to make decisions that protect both of you. Never allow someone else to take charge of your protection. And further still, the last thing we need is more babies being brought into the world before we are ready to give them love, attention, and all the other things they deserve and need. (Diapers cost a lot of money!)

Let's face it—mistakes can happen in every area of your life. Aside from sex, I have made varying degrees of mistakes in different areas of my life: school, friendships, family, and career. And unfortunately, some accidents and mistakes you cannot fix or take back; they are lasting and permanent.

There is a particular accident from my childhood that I will never forget, and I want to share it because the experience proved to me that some mistakes are permanent. And I tell you this story so that you don't have to make permanent mistakes like I have made, such as this one. I was twelve years old, and it was Christmas break. My older brother Harry and I were on my grandfather's farm in Iowa for the holiday. We both loved the Dallas Cowboys and we were proudly wearing our jerseys. Our older cousin was seventeen, and he and his family lived in another house on the farm. The three of us came up with the brilliant idea that we should have a BB gun fight. I was the brash smart-ass youngest, and I said it should be those two against me. We put on layers and layers of clothes so the high-powered BB rifles wouldn't cause too much pain, never thinking to protect our heads. We started to battle, those two shooting at me and me at them. I hunkered down next to the barn, popping up to fire off a few shots whenever I could. They ducked behind a boat on a trailer rig forty feet away. I still see what happened next in slow motion. My brother popped his head up to see where I was just as I looked out to shoot them. I took aim, pulled the trigger and heard dead silence. Everything stopped. Then I heard a scream. I ran over to see my brother's eye dripping blood and mucus, staining his hands and his Dallas Cowboys jersey. I had accidentally shot my brother in the eye. It may have been an accident, but stupidity and recklessness was the cause. My brother had surgery and lost his eye, and to this day he wears a prosthesis.

I have spent many days replaying the events, thinking "if only" we had not been playing with BB guns, or if we had worn protective head coverings, or if I had pointed the gun a few centimeters in another direction, things would have been different.

> *Mistakes are decisions we have control over.*

Even though I know what happened with my brother was a freak accident, I wish I had made choices that would have led to a different outcome. And I hope that in your life you will make the best choices and avoid mistakes. It is often hard to separate an accident—something you have little or no control over—from a mistake—a more conscious act where you have the information to make the right decision but you choose to either ignore that information or knowingly make a wrong decision. Mistakes are decisions we have control over. And you can make a mistake in an instant, which is why it's important to know who you are and what you stand for before you find yourself in a situation where you make a wrong decision. Choosing to drop out of school is a mistake—we all know the consequences, and yet every year hundreds of thousands of kids choose to drop out of school. Having unprotected sex is a mistake too—and you knew the consequences, yet you chose to do it anyway. A positive, responsible decision is to stay in school and figure out a way to make it work for you. Like finding another school if the one you are currently enrolled in doesn't fit with you. Or even changing your classes in the school you attend. And a positive, responsible decision about sex is to wait until you are ready and prepared to be responsible.

Just because you love something and want to be successful at it doesn't mean you are immune to making mistakes in that area. As you know, I love acting, but I can even point out times when I have made some big mistakes in my career.

For example, it took a long time for me to realize that old adage my grandmother would say actually holds true over time: "A bird in the hand is worth two in the bush." Sometimes you have to be happy with where you are and what you have. All we really have is this moment, right now, so we have to be careful not to walk away from blessings, thinking that there is another blessing around the corner. In 2001, I was doing a successful run of a play in New York City called *Blue*, costarring Phylicia Rashad, who played my mother. We played to sold-out houses nearly every night. And one day, about three months into the run, I got a call from my agent who told me about this movie, 8 Mile, that Eminem was going to do. He said that it was going to be the biggest movie of the year and there was a role that was perfect for me. I auditioned for Curtis Hanson, the director of 8 Mile, in New York City, and shortly thereafter they told my agent they wanted me to fly to Detroit to work with Eminem for two days. I told them that it was impossible because I get only one day off a week from the play, and the theater hadn't hired an understudy. My agent called me back and said, "Are you crazy? This movie is going to be huge. It will make you a star! If you have to leave the play, so be it." They said they wanted to make a deal for me to be in the movie and that when I went to Detroit I would sign my contract, but they wouldn't officially hire me unless I came to work with Eminem for two days. I thought, "This is a huge opportunity," so I went to the artistic director of the theater and said I would be leaving the show. He was hurt and upset, but rather than close the show, they decided to train someone to replace me. On September 9, 2001, I flew to Detroit, Michigan.

All day on the 10th, Eminem and I rehearsed scenes from the movie. It went great, I was charged and excited. The next morning was supposed to be the final screen test. As I was getting ready to do my best work, the phone in my hotel room rang and someone said, "Screen test is canceled." I asked, "Why?" They said, "Haven't you watched the news?" And I said, "No. I've been focused on preparing for the screen test." They just said, "Turn on the TV." We all know what happened on September 11, 2001. I, like everyone else, sat watching the TV. Sitting in my hotel room, I really didn't know what to do. I was in Detroit, alone, and all the planes were grounded indefinitely. So I decided to make my way to one of the car rental places at the airport. I rented a car and began a miserable drive, by myself, from Detroit to Los Angeles. A day and half into the drive, as my cell phone was about to die, I got a call from my agent. He said I wouldn't be getting the role in 8 *Mile*. The studio decided to go with a bigger name. That drive was perhaps the most miserable and lonely drive of my life for many reasons, not the least being the devastation of what had happened on September 11. Not only did I fail to get the role in 8 *Mile*, I had walked away from a wonderful and successful play in New York City and had disappointed a group of people I respected at the theater. I felt like I had made the dumbest mistake anyone could make. Rather than appreciating what I had, I was just looking for the next best thing. What I've learned is that oftentimes, the best thing is what you have right now. So enjoy all the great things in your life right now and don't feel that you have to rush into anything that may lead to a mistake.

> Oftentimes, the best thing is what you have right now.

It seems a recurring theme in the letters we have exchanged has been your making the transition from boyhood to manhood. It is important you understand that there is no age associated with that transition; meaning, there are plenty of forty-year-olds still living in the boyhood phase of their life. They make childish choices and do not take on the responsibilities of manhood. They are forty and haven't even made the transition into being a grown-up. On the other hand, there are some young dudes I've met who have been forced to make the transition into manhood much earlier than they wanted or should have had to; as early as twelve or thirteen years old.

I would prefer that you choose not to have sex at this point in your life, but that's your choice to make. I have repeatedly said I would always have your back, and I'm not going to disappear just because you didn't follow my advice. But, listen very closely to what I'm about to tell you. If you are going to choose to participate in "adult" or "manhood" based activities, like having sex or driving a car, then you have to be responsible in your choices regarding those activities. Like I've said to you before, no matter what you choose to do in your life, if you are going to do it, then do it the right way. Sex requires adult, responsible choices. So no more mistakes of a sexual nature, please.

And on that note, now that you know all my bizness. I've got to go, because I've invited this girl over for dinner tonight. And no, we are not having sex. Men and women can hang out without having to fool around. Ya' heard? Hit me back when you can. Grace, Peace, and Blessings.

Your Friend,

Hill

---------Original Message----------

From: Young_Brotha@home.net
Date: November 22, 2005 6:06 PM
To: Hill@manifestyourdestiny.net
Subject: HIV/AIDS

Hill, my friends told me that AIDS is not really a big deal anymore. Since I'm not part of a high-risk group (I'm not gay or a drug user), do I really need to worry about AIDS?

Date: November 24, 2005 7:48 PM
From: Hill@manifestyourdestiny.net
To: Young_Brotha@home.net
Subject: Fwd: Re: HIV/AIDS

I am not an expert on HIV and AIDS; however, I do know someone who is. I'm going to forward your e-mail to Phill Wilson, executive director of The Black AIDS Institute.

HH

---------Begin Forwarded Message----------

I'm glad you've raised this question. Like your friends, there are many people who don't think AIDS is a big deal anymore. Unfortunately, they are wrong. You don't have to be gay or a drug user to get infected with HIV. HIV transmission is really easy to understand.

AIDS is a blood-borne disease, so if you are sexually active with another person, and that person has HIV, you are at risk if you don't protect yourself. And the only way for you to know if the other person is infected is for the two of you to get tested for HIV. And that's what I would recommend you do.

You might want to tell your friends that over half of the over-all new AIDS cases in America are among African-Americans, and most important, blacks make up 56 percent of the new AIDS cases among young people.

So, if you choose to be sexually active, and you really don't want to worry about HIV, you should make sure you use protection every time.

—Phill Wilson,
The Black AIDS Institute

Part Four

Dreams and Aspirations:
Making it Happen

MANifest Your Destiny

Dreaming Big

I dream for a living.
STEVEN SPIELBERG

December 1, 2005
New York

Dear Young Brotha,

I'm writing you back from the set of a film I'm working on. It's called *Premium,* and we're shooting a night scene in Brooklyn. It's 3:00 A.M., and I'm waiting for the crew to finish lighting the set so we can shoot. One of the movie's lighting technicians just said something that made me think of you, and I wanted to pass it on. He started talking to me about happiness and what it means to be happy in one's life. He said that even though it was three in the morning, and he was bone tired from working these crazy long hours on the movie, he was still happy, because he was doing what he wanted to do. He was simply fulfilling his dreams; but he also said it isn't easy. A lot of people don't think there's a difference between "simple" and "easy," but there's a huge difference. He explained that it's a "simple" choice for him to work on movies and do what he loves, but most times it's a lot of work and, therefore, it's not "easy."

In my first letter to you I said that I want you to be "unreasonably happy" in your life. In order to achieve that, I need you to dream big, and then get to work fulfilling those dreams. In doing so, I believe it will make you "unreasonably happy." "But how do I get there?" you asked me in your last letter. My lighting technician's story gives a hint to the answer. How do any of us fulfill our dreams? It's simple, but it's not easy.

The simple answer of how you fulfill your dreams is, you believe. That's it. You dream big and believe you can do it. You believe you will do it. But then, that begs the question, what is "it"? "It" is anything you want "it" to be. You can be a great rapper and a great student. You can be popular and get good grades. You can just chill in the cut and write the next great American novel. You can even use a pen name and no one ever has to know that you wrote it. Then you can sit back and collect the checks. If you truly believe you can, you can. And check this out—belief works in both positive and negative directions. If, for some reason, some part of you wants your "it" to be prison, then you can and probably will make that happen too.

> *It's simple, but it's not easy.*

Back in the day, I had a dream of being a great rapper. One of the rhymes I wrote when I was in high school was: "Goals and dreams are one in the same, just say you believe and both you will attain." I was right on point with that rhyme, and knowing what your goals and dreams are is the simple part.

You've been telling me that your only goal and dream is to make lots of money. We talked about this already but it must not be sinking in. So let me set you straight—making money is not a goal. Making money is a result. Now, there is nothing wrong with making lots of money. I make lots of money. And I like making lots of money. But making money in and of itself is not a goal. If your only goal is to make money, you will always be controlled by your desire for money instead of you controlling money. One key to controlling your relationship with money is to first connect with the things you love to do, and then have faith that in pursuing the things you love, you will eventually make money. Ordering your priorities that way ensures that the pursuit of money is kept in its proper perspective—as a result of a goal and not the goal itself.

A lot of young brothas have never been taught that in order to know what your dreams are you have to ask yourself questions—questions like: "What do I really really like?" Not what have I become comfortable liking but "What do I like for real?" You've said to me before that you like your PlayStation 2 or your music videos. But that's not really what you like. That is just "stuff." If you go further and dig a little deeper inside yourself, and you ask, "What warms me inside?" "What feeds me?" "What do I really connect to?" you're gonna find answers that have less to do with things and stuff and more to do with motivation and purpose.

What do I mean by that? Here's an example. A lot of people approach me and say, "It must be cool doing movies and being on TV every week; you must be able to buy anything you want." But what they don't realize is that, for me, what's great about acting is not the "things" or "stuff" I can buy. For me, I love the art of portraying a character that makes people laugh, cry, think, feel, or just escape for a bit. Your "purpose" is to do what you love and follow your dreams. It's as simple as that. However, truly living your life that way is not always easy; it takes hard work.

Don't get me wrong, it took me a while to find what my purpose was and what dreams I wanted to pursue, and many experiences contributed to that discovery. The summer between my junior and senior years in high school, I was invited to a student government leadership seminar at Stanford University. A dynamic motivational speaker named John Alston walked into a classroom and handed me a workbook full of questions I had never thought to ask myself—questions like, "How do you see your walk on this earth?" "Where do you fit in?" "What are you passionate about?" "What makes your heart beat faster?" I never knew, but the answers to these questions were inside me all along, and all it took was someone that I respected to ask them of me. Looking back, I feel that my answers to those questions commenced a new journey for me. So what are your answers to those questions. Think about it.

One thing I want to point out is that sometimes God and the universe will make you passionate about one thing that ultimately will help lead you to your dreams. For instance, for me, when I was in high school I was an all-county receiver and defensive back in football and dreamed of being a pro football player. I was the only player on my team who had run, thrown, caught, and intercepted balls for touchdowns. I truly believed that it was my purpose and dream to play in the NFL. My passion for football led me down the path to what I would ultimately find to be my true purpose. How? Well, if I hadn't aspired to being the best football player I could be and dreamed of playing in the pros, I would not have become all-county and I would not have been recruited to attend Brown University. At Brown I gained some great experiences but also took a random class that changed the entire direction of my life: acting. Looking back today I can see that everything in our life happens for a reason. There are no coincidences. The only thing we need to do is to be purposeful with the choices we make as we pursue our dreams and to stay open to signs when the universe is trying to get our attention. I define faith as the combination of belief and trust. I therefore ask that you have faith in wholeheartedly following your dreams, because following those dreams will ultimately lead you to your purpose. I promise.

Check it out—it's all about dreaming big and working hard. First, I want you to dream big. No, bigger! Bigger! Okay. That's a start. Think of a dream right now, however crazy and out there, and then I want you to imagine yourself doing it. For example, inventing the coolest video game that anyone ever played or owning your own NFL team or being president of the United States. Now imagine yourself working hard to do it. If you imagined being president, think of the steps you might take to get there. Like first volunteering to work on a political campaign of a local politician and then running for a local office

> Dream big and believe you can do it.

yourself, like city councilman; then running for a bigger office like congressman; working in congress, creating laws that make people's lives better and on and on until you are the prez. It's possible, as is anything you can dare to imagine! There is power in visualization, but you truly have to believe in your soul that you will accomplish it. Then, you'll have to work hard to achieve it, and working hard is *simple* when you enjoy what you are doing; get it? For example, I work very hard as an actor, countless auditions, character preparation, research, line memorization, rehearsal, and long shooting days, but all of that is simple because I love what I do. So do I mind getting up at five in the morning and working until midnight only to do it again the next day? No, I don't ever mind, because I am doing what I am passionate about. That's it. You feel me? Dream big, work hard, and believe.

Now, I bet you are saying, "Yo, I can dream big. Hell, I got that down. But, I don't know about that 'work hard' stuff." Here's another little secret I'm gonna hip you to, okay? If you find what you love to do then, 'hard work' becomes easy—it's more fun than just chillin' or doing some job just for the money. If you're doing something you love, working hard at it is more fun than working just to work; now *that's* hard! And don't think it's just me that feels this way. Tiger Woods said, "I get to play golf for a living. What more can you ask for—getting paid for doing what you love." So given that, the question that you have to answer right here, right now, is—what do you love to do?

Me, I love to act, and I want to do whatever it takes to best portray the character I am playing. For instance, a few years ago I did a movie called *The Visit*, where I played a character who was in prison and dying of AIDS. To prepare for the film I began doing a great deal of research: interviewing inmates and speaking with many people who had AIDS. The director and I would spend hours and hours rehearsing. From my research, the director and I decided that I should try to physically represent my character's deterioration toward death by trying to lose thirty pounds over the course of the shooting of the movie. The director agreed to shoot the film in chronological order so that at the beginning of the film I could look healthy and by the end look totally skinny and sick. It was hard work to keep shooting the movie while losing the weight. There were many days in a row where I ate no food at all, I only drank water. I was so hungry. I would get light-headed and sometimes forgot my lines. Even though it was hard work to transform myself, I loved it because I was acting in a great movie and playing a character that I was passionate about. I'll tell you more about being passionate in life in my next letter.

Working hard doing something you enjoy makes you feel more vibrant and more alive. It's like when I'm playing a video game, and I'm playing hard, and I'm at the most challenging level and I'm hitting keys fast; I'm focused. That's more fun than playing an unchallenging game at a ho-hum level. The same is true for living life. But living life is just like in a video game; you gotta stay in it. You gotta stay in the game while you follow your dreams. Remember I wrote you a whole letter about "staying in the game?" Working hard while you are in the game is equally important.

Hey, I just realized that exactly fifty years ago today, Rosa Parks, who recently passed away, refused to give up her seat on a bus in Alabama. Many people believe that this act of defiance by a true American hero sparked the beginning of the civil rights movement. Being a hero in the struggle for civil rights was Rosa Parks's destiny. By doing one courageous act, she helped shape this country. That is what "MANifesting Your Destiny" is all about. I'll tell you more about that in another letter.

Getting back to "working hard," they are calling me in to shoot the last scene of this movie. Have a great day Young Brotha. Write me back soon. Grace, Peace, and Blessings! One.

Your Friend,

Hill

----------Original Message----------

From: Young_Brotha@home.net
Date: December 9, 2005 11:02 PM
To: Hill@manifestyourdestiny.net
Subject: Superstardom

Hill, how do I become a superstar at something, and if I want to be a superstar rapper or athlete, why should I have to go to school?

Date: December 10, 2005 8:57 AM
From: Hill@manifestyourdestiny.net
To: Young_Brotha@home.net
Subject: Fwd: Re: Superstardom

I thought the best person to answer your question would be a superstar athlete. So I forwarded your e-mail to the superstar tennis player Venus Williams. Here's her response.

HH

----------Begin Forwarded Message----------

School is a very important part of becoming a superstar. Education can be gained in various ways and all your options should be explored. My definition of a "superstar" is anyone who excels beyond the average person and has mastered his or her craft. To master your craft you must be focused, passionate, and practice tirelessly to achieve perfection. You must also treat your body like a temple with exercise and healthy food. It is also important to expand your knowledge of the world you live in. Whether you are an athlete, actor, or politician, reading, traveling, and learning new languages can help make you a better YOU!

Good Luck, Venus Williams

Living with Passion

I am having the ride of my life right now. . . . I wish I could take what I'm feeling right now and put it in the water system, and we would love each other a whole lot more.
JAMIE FOXX

December 16, 2005
Mexico City

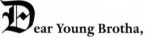ear Young Brotha,

I'm here in Mexico, and I'm about to go on a sightseeing tour to see the ancient Aztec city of Teotihuacán. It has the third-largest pyramid in the world. I've heard so many stories about what a brilliant culture the Native Americans created. It's fascinating to see and learn about it firsthand. I wish I could speak Spanish. I think learning that language is going to be next on my "To Do" list. Do you speak any other languages besides English? I want to learn as many languages as I can; that's one of my passions. It's amazing to me what this brilliant culture was able to create without the help of machines or electricity, or any of the modern things we use to build things today. We could learn so much from looking back on the past, and that goes for all areas of our lives.

For me, I am a better actor because I always study the greats who have come before me, the Denzel Washingtons, Marlon Brandos, Meryl Streeps, Michael Peñas, and Morgan Freemans. I found out that all people who have ever achieved their dreams had one thing in common. They have *passion*. Neil Armstrong was passionate about space travel. Denzel is passionate about acting, and me, I am passionate about *you* finding your passion. Just like I wrote about in my last letter about dreams, most of us are afraid even to ask ourselves what we are passionate about. But for real—what makes you smile? What makes your heart beat faster? What makes you excited? I'm not talking about that hot girl that works at the mall. I'm talking about a different kind of excited. Remember, there is no wrong answer. There is only your truth.

When I was eighteen years old, I went off to college and had no idea what I was passionate about. I really had no idea. If someone asked me, "What do you want to do or be?" I would always make something up or just say, "A professional football player." But I didn't know. That's what is great about going to college and getting an education. It gives you time and a chance to explore things you might not even know you are passionate about. That's what happened to me. My first semester freshman year, I needed a class that met on Tuesdays and Thursdays and got out before 3:30 because I was on the football team and had to make it to practice on time. Looking through the available class catalog I saw a class that met

> *What makes your heart beat faster?*

the days and times I needed to fill: Theater Arts 21—Voice for the Actor: Shakespeare, taught by Professor Barbara Tannenbaum. Did I have any idea that walking into that classroom would change the direction of my life? Absolutely not. There's no reason I should have had any idea, because it's very rare that we are aware that divinity is blessing us the exact moment it's happening.

I didn't realize it at the time, but God and the universe conspired to change my life, right at that moment—introducing me to a new path; a new journey. In that class, I found that I had a passion for the art of acting. I found that the more I did it, the more I wanted to do it. I found that it was something I wanted to do, simply because I loved doing it—not to be able to buy nice things with the money I might, possibly, someday make doing it. I wanted to do it because I loved doing it at that moment, right then, right there. I found something I was motivated about. I found my purpose. In the beginning, people were far from encouraging about me following my passion. Instead they projected their own fears onto me, often saying things like "Be prepared to stay broke," or "It's hard to make a living acting," or "That's a great hobby, but get a real job." What they didn't realize is that I wasn't motivated by the money because I had found my purpose; the thing I was born to do. Guess what happened? The more I pursued my passion, the more opportunities to make money followed. It happened to me and it will happen to you too.

Acting makes my heart beat faster. When I play characters that make people laugh, cry, think, or just escape, I am happy and excited. That is my passion. But passion doesn't have to be reflected solely in what you do for a living. You can take passionate interest in many things. I am also passionate about art, yet I am probably the worse painter known to man, so I collect paintings, photographs, and sculptures that move me. I'm also passionate about traveling. I have been to Japan, two countries in Africa, South America, Mexico, and nine countries in Europe. Those are just a few of my passions. What are yours? Write what you are passionate about on a piece of paper. All my life I've been passionate about sports. When I didn't have a dime, I could watch a game on the television, pop some popcorn, make a hotdog, and be blissed out. Passion is about this inner excitement for something bubbling to the surface. You don't have to be rich to be passionate about something; you just have to be undeniably excited.

I guess what I'm trying to say is, you like having fun, right? Well, so do I. It is much more fun and rewarding to allow yourself to live passionately and with unbridled enthusiasm than to walk through life without passion "trying to get by." People who live their lives with passion never "get by." Instead, they thrive, often living beyond their dreams. Why do you think ballplayers yell and scream when they win a championship? Tiger Woods pumps his fist, Lance Armstrong raises his arms in his yellow jersey, Terrell Owens does a dance in the end zone, and LeBron James slaps the backboard and hollas after a nasty dunk. Even Donald Trump gets excited when he closes a big deal. Passion is fun. When I talk about passion I think of L.A. Reid, CEO of Arista Records, one of the most powerful men in the music industry. L.A. Reid admits to being an overachiever. I read where he said, "I want to do more, more, and more. Better, better, and better. I'm passionate about working with so many creative people, whether it is

> *I like getting excited about what I do every day.*

my artists or producers or executives. I really enjoy having huge challenges and figuring out ways to accomplish it all without ever sacrificing the quality of what we do."

I like getting excited about what I do every day. It is fun to be excited, to say, "Let's do this. Let's do this life thing. Let's do this happiness thing!" It's cool, fine, and fun to be crazy passionate. You know, Beyoncé and Jay-Z had that song "Crazy in Love." There's nothing wrong with being crazy in love with your life. Remember, you are not doing this alone. I am proud to be your older brother dedicated to helping you, Young Brotha, find your passion.

Oh, I forgot to tell you, before I came down here to Mexico, I bumped into my man Jay-Z. I know you like him, so I included a picture of us in the letter. Hope you like it. I'll be home for a few days then I'm headed to Aspen, Colorado, to visit my mom, and I want to get your letter before I break out. Grace, Peace, and Blessings my Brotha! One.

Your Friend,

Hill

----------Original Message----------

From: Young_Brotha@home.net
Date: December 22, 2005 5:55 PM
To: Hill@manifestyourdestiny.net
Subject: Questions

Hill, you said it's important to ask myself questions to learn more about myself and what I am passionate about. I don't understand. What are some questions I can ask myself?

Date: December 23, 2005 11:08 AM
From: Hill@manifestyourdestiny.net
To: Young_brother@home.net
Subject: Re: Questions

Here are some of the questions that I've learned to ask myself. Take out a pen and write down your answers.

What makes you happy?

What are you really truly afraid of? Seriously, what makes you scared?

What are your hopes?

What gives you inspiration?

What makes you stop doing things?

What is it about a girl that makes you like her? Be honest with yourself!

If you like video games, why do you play them? What is it about them that you like?

If you like hip-hop and rap, what is it about them that you like?

Deep down, who do you really look up to? (Don't give me the answer that you think is the correct answer, but for real, who do you look up to?)

What is it about that person that makes you look up to them?

Are there elements in you that you see similar to the person you look up to?

Does the life of the person you look up to look like the life you want to have?

Remember, there are no right or wrong answers.

What you've written is just information for you and how you see yourself. The life that you're living now and your answers give hints about where you're headed in the future. Life is an evolving journey. Just like the weather, every day is a little bit different than the next. That means that every day your answers to many of the above questions may change. And that's cool too. Priorities change. Desires change. Goals change. Dreams change. And the way we go about achieving what makes us happy changes. And that's the way it should be. But the answers to these questions give you an idea—or what I call a template—as to where you are *right now*, and where your head is at right now. It's just information, man. But, like I've said, what we *do* with the information is the most important piece of the puzzle.

HH

MANifesting Your Destiny

I was forced to be an artist and a CEO from the beginning,
so I was forced to be like a businessman because when I was trying to
get a record deal, it was so hard to get a record deal on my own that it
was either give up or create my own company.
JAY-Z

January 1, 2006
Aspen, Colorado

Dear Young Brotha,

Hey man, I'm here in Aspen, Colorado, surrounded by snowcapped mountains. I just finished hitting the slopes and talking to the "snow-honeys" in the lodge, and it's New Year's Day. Happy New Year, Young Brotha! I love you. It's going to be a great year, for both of us. Know that.

I'm a little sad right now, because I just found out that a friend of mine, Tyrone, won't be coming back for Shining Stars week this year. Shining Stars is a thing they do in Aspen where they bring underprivileged kids with cancer here to learn to ski and play in the snow. I just found out that Young Brotha Tyrone passed away. It made me miss him and at the same time it made me want to connect with you. I needed to make sure that you, the newest perfect model, are working to-ward being unreason-ably happy today. I know that many of the children with cancer won't beat the odds, but I hope and pray they will anyway. Besides, you never know when a miracle will happen.

> You never know when a miracle will happen.

Tyrone was eighteen years old, and taught everyone he met how to be a fighter. He lived all his life in Denver, so he had seen plenty of snow, but he'd never had a chance to ski. He arrived bald-headed from chemotherapy, a big smile on his face, and announced that he intended to learn to ski in one day. He lived every day as if it were his last. Tyrone's nurse had to make him slow down so he wouldn't get worn out the first day. All week he put his heart and soul into mas-tering the sport. On race day, he came in second, losing to a boy who grew up skiing. Young Brotha Tyrone counted that as a win, and it was.

You know how I've written to you about staying focused and being fearlessly present in each moment? Well, Tyrone lived that principle. He loved every minute of skiing and he joined in every activity with that same fearless enthusiasm. He lived the way I want to see you live: passionately! His life was short yet he squeezed pleasure out of every minute. Peo-ple would look at him and say "How could he be happy? That's unreasonable." Tyrone personified being unreason-ably happy. I loved Tyrone and his spirit. He inspired me and everyone he met not to make excuses and to live fully. Just like I've been asking you to do in my letters, he dreamed big and lived those dreams. He didn't just "try," he "did." You and I, all of us, have some of Tyrone's spirit in us. We have to bring it out.

In my last letter to you I asked you the same important questions I ask myself: "What do you dream about?" "What are your goals?" "How do you see your life unfolding?" "Where do you see yourself in the next year?" "The next five years?" Your response to me was, "I don't know." But you know I'm not gonna let you off the hook that easy. You do know the answers to my questions. The answers are already inside of you. How do I know that? Because the universe has already provided a preordained destiny for you that is yours, and yours alone. It's like a fingerprint: No two are alike. Your destiny is unique to you and it is only through specifically answering those questions that you allow the universe to help you achieve your dreams. That is what MANifesting your destiny is—answering questions like those above and then taking the steps to put into action the thing you were born to do.

It is usually our fears that won't allow us to access the answers that are already inside of our hearts and minds. That fear creates a challenge for us, doesn't it? But for you to truly MANifest your destiny, you'll need to go beyond even what your mind can think. Bill Gates, for example, created Microsoft out of his imagination, and it became one of the most successful and powerful companies in the world, and has changed the way we all live and do business. Microsoft inspired computer experts Sergey Brin and Larry Page to create Google, a superinformation highway that may one day become more influential and more powerful than Microsoft. In their creations, they were truly MANifesting their destinies. And I am in your life right now to help you MANifest yours.

All great inventions began with a single idea in someone's mind: the lightbulb, the car, the microchip, baseball, chess, electricity, shoes, peanut butter, and so on. They are all things that never existed before someone invented them. There's a popular old quote that says, "If you can dream it or think it, you can do it." I want us to take that to the next level. I want us to figure out how you can create a life beyond even what your mind may be able to think or dream possible. That would be you truly MANifesting your destiny. Even Michael Jordan agrees, saying, "You have to expect great things of yourself before you can do them."

I'll give you an example. A buddy I went to Harvard Law School with is a man named Barack Obama. Seven years ago, Barack decided he wanted to be a U.S. congressman from his district in the city of Chicago. Yeah, that's a great goal. Be a congressman. Guess what happened? He ran for congress, and was completely and soundly defeated. Was he sad? Yes. Was he disappointed? For a little while, yes, he was disappointed because he lost. His goal, his dream, was to be a congressman, and he failed. However that loss didn't stop him from continuing to pursue his dreams in politics. He decided to work even harder and ran for an even bigger office.

> *God and the universe have much more planned for you than you can even imagine.*

Fast-forward, six years later, and today, he is only the third African-American U.S. senator in history. He represents the entire state of Illinois and our great country all over the world. He was the keynote speaker at the 2004 Democratic National Convention. His name is now on the lips of the most powerful people in America. Not only did Barack reach his goal, he went far beyond it. Being a member of the U.S. Senate is a much, much bigger deal than being a U.S. representative in the House. He is in such an influential position, people are now talking about him one day being president of the United States. He told me that if he had won that congressional election seven years ago, today he would be a no-name junior congressman, struggling to stay elected. He proves that God and the universe have much more planned for you than you can even imagine. Do you see what I'm saying? The universe had a bigger plan for him than even he had for himself. If he had taken that first loss personally, he might have given up and not lived the bigger better dream the universe had in store for him.

So how does Barack's story relate to you? He's a great example of a man who dreamed big, followed through, and did so with passion. And by doing all of this he was fulfilling his destiny in life. I'm here to tell you that God and the universe have much more in store for you and much more planned for you than you can ever dream of or imagine possible. In order for that to take effect, you have to first, dream; and second, work hard to achieve those dreams. Barack would not be a U.S. senator today if he had not run and lost the election for Congress. Losing was a blessing for him, but he had to run and work hard to have that blessing take effect. Rather than giving up when he lost, he took the lessons he learned from his defeat and worked even harder. My friend Matt has a saying that kind of illustrates this point as well. He says, "With a little bit of persistence and some common sense, sometimes you can get the thing you're chasing, even if it doesn't exist." That holds true for every aspect of your life. Family. Friends. School. Career. Even girls. To MANifest your destiny, you must take action in life. That "action" is what the "doing-ness of life" is all about.

All right, I've gotta run, we'll pick that subject up in my next letter. This fine honey I met on the slopes wants to have some hot chocolate, so I said I'd meet her at the ski lodge. Hit me back. We'll talk soon. Be well. Grace, Peace, and Blessings my Young Brotha!

Your Friend,

Hill

----------Original Message----------

From: Young_Brotha@home.net
Date: January 7, 2006 10:32 PM
To: Hill@manifestyourdestiny.net
Subject: Smoking and Drinking

Hill, I don't really like alcohol or smoking anyway, but why do a lot of people say smoking and drinking are so bad?

Date: January 8, 2006 2:30 AM
From: Hill@manifestyourdestiny.net
To: Young_Brotha@home.net
Subject: Re: Smoking and Drinking

Because they *are* bad for your body. The nicotine in tobacco and the alcohol in drinks harm your liver, heart, and brain. Also, some people get drunk, start fights, get into accidents, or beat up on other people.

To be more specific, I know that a lot people lump smoking and drinking together. They say, "Don't smoke. Don't drink." But smoking and drinking are two different things. First of all, neither one is really natural. Smoking is just what it is; it's putting toxic smoke into your lungs. Our lungs are made to receive air, not smoke. Now, drinking can damage your liver, but the biggest problems with drinking are the negative results and actions that come when people drink too much. The worst being those who choose to drive after they've been drinking. Not only can they kill themselves, but worse still, kill others quite easily. You've heard me say before that it doesn't tend to be our actions that get us into trouble, but our reactions that get us into trouble, and it's how your mind and body react under the influence of alcohol that often can cause problems.

Now the problem with smoking is that over the long haul it just tears your body up. It's almost like putting slow poison into your system. And if you're going to truly MANifest your destiny, you have to be around and healthy for the long haul. Feel me? E-mail me back when you get a chance.

HH

Fear and the "Doing-Ness" of Life

If you're not frightened that you might fail, you'll never do the job. If you're frightened, you'll work like crazy.

CESAR CHAVEZ

February 1, 2006
Chicago, Illinois

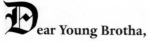ear Young Brotha,

Hey Man. I'm writing this in a hotel room in Chicago. I'm in town speaking on a panel for the Chicago International Film Festival. It's ironic that in the letter I just received you wrote about feeling alone in the world. Hotels can be very lonely places, especially when you're away from home and away from your family and friends. I can't tell you the number of times being alone in a hotel room has made me feel lonely. Luckily, I get to write you a letter, which always makes me aware of how blessed I am to have you as my young brotha and friend.

You sounded kind of down in your last letter. You said

school is "all right," and your mom is "all right." Everything is just "all right." One of the things I've learned to do when I'm down is to turn the focus away from what I feel bad about and concentrate on what is going well in my life. So, I take the time to write a gratitude list. This list includes all the things and people in my life that make me feel good, like my friendships, family, and the simple fact that I can walk, talk, and see. Sometimes I also write poems because if I write about what makes me feel sad, it often helps the sadness go away. You can also write these things in a journal. It's okay to be a man who keeps a journal—the coolest dudes I know all keep journals. Stop what you are doing right now and write down three things you are grateful about. Now, focus on those three things. Breathe. You'll feel just a tiny bit better. Try doing that once a day. Add three more things to your gratitude list. In a month you'll be amazed by how long that list has become.

I know it's hard to be hyped and enthusiastic all the time. Energy, like everything in life, tends to ebb and flow. In my last letter I asked what you wanted and you kept saying, "I'm trying to do this," or "I'm trying to make such and such happen." Hearing you respond with that language kind of disappointed me, which may come as a surprise to you. But "trying" is a curse word. You and I are "do-ers," we are not "*trying* to do-ers." Hear me?

Your "life" isn't passive. Even if you're trying to make it passive, life is not passive. By that, I mean that even if you try not to be noticed, to do nothing, to lie up in your room with your head under your covers, whatever choice you make, life will provide a reaction to that choice that will keep you from being passive. If you decide to sit on your couch and not move, life will eventually make you hungry and thirsty, and eventually you will have to get up and get something to eat and drink.

Life is active, not passive. You and I are not going to have regrets because we are

Your life isn't passive.

going to act on our intuition. That is the doing-ness of life. Even Nike tried to sell sneakers based on this by marketing the phrase, "Just Do It." You and I analyze a situation, work past our fears, and then we take action. There's an old saying, "There are three kinds of people: Those who make things happen; those who wait for things to happen; and those who sit and wonder what happened." We make things happen. We're not just trying to do life, we're *going* to do it!

What is at work in your life that makes you think you should be passive? Do you know? It's fear. My cousin, Reverend Michael, describes fear as "False Evidence Appearing Real." People say to me, "Aren't you afraid knowing you are acting in front of millions of people every week?" If it were the old Hill, I probably wouldn't be able to be an actor, let alone on *CSI: NY*. But today I know the only things worth having are those that take you out of your "comfort zone" and make you truly afraid. Let's start talking about what your fears are, Young Brotha. Fear is nothing but a messed up four-letter word trying to take you and me away from our destinies.

I know many young brothas who can't speak of their destiny or dreams because there's a voice that pops up; a voice of doubt that tells them it will never happen. "Doubt" and "fear" are close relatives. A lot of young brothas deny they have fear. For instance, I know you, and I know that you're saying right now, "Come on Hill, I ain't afraid of nothing." Don't try and front on me; we've been telling too many truths in these letters to punk out now. We all have fears. It's like when you told me how cool you thought it would be to learn photography, and I found some local classes you could take that were in your budget. When I asked whether you had followed up you said, "Naw, I really didn't want to." You were passive. What you were really saying is that you were afraid to put yourself in the uncomfortable position of joining a class where you wouldn't know anyone, and trying something so new.

There is an amazing quote that I think all young brothas should post next to their beds and recite after a moment of peaceful breathing when they wake up. It can be used as a daily mantra to ground you and release fear and negative thoughts before you begin your day and put you on a productive path. Read these words and let them sink in slowly, "Our deepest fear is not that we are inadequate; our deepest fear is that we are powerful beyond measure." Although Marianne Williamson, the spiritual teacher, actually wrote this, it is usually attributed to Nelson Mandela because he recited it in a speech and it had a profound effect on people. Fear is natural; it's just not real. Letting our fears and, subsequently, our doubts, stop us

> *Fear is natural.*
> *It's just not real.*

from achieving our dreams and goals is not natural; it's a cop-out. I have always been afraid of failure. I have always been terrified that I wouldn't be good enough. In the past, if I didn't know for sure I would be successful at something, I wouldn't even try it. That voice was my fear MANifesting doubt. That MANifested in my life by me putting off doing my schoolwork or putting off talking to a girl that I had a crush on or putting off my weight training for the football team, because I doubted whether I was going to be considered "the best." What's messed up about how I acted is that it guaranteed my never being the best because my fears and doubts made me a huge procrastinator. My fears and doubts became self-fulfilling prophecies. It took my asking myself hard questions about why I didn't take a particular action that I knew I should have taken to begin to win the battle against my fears—for instance, in high school when I asked myself why I didn't participate in student government even though I wanted to. I had to admit that I was afraid no one would vote for me. I also was terrified of public speaking. Eventually I confronted those fears and became student body vice president. I often wonder if I would have been able to have become an actor without challenging my fears in high school.

When I e-mailed you and asked, "What scares you?" you replied, "Asking girls out." When I read your reply, I had to laugh because it amazes me how alike we are. Look, I have been there myself. Just like you, my voice of doubt and fear comes up with girls all the time. I might meet a really cool girl and like her, but she has the power to reject me, so it's hard to ask her out on a date. If it's a girl that I don't like as much, she is much easier to ask out. Why do you think that is? It's because, with the girl I really like, I care about the result, and my fear level rises.

Let me give you an example. Do you remember the singer Aaliyah? I thought she was so beautiful, talented, and nice. I would see her around every once in a while. One time, we were both at a party at Leonardo DiCaprio's house. We were hanging out talking and she was there with her friend. I wanted to ask Aaliyah out, or at least get her phone number, but I kept hesitating. I kept getting nervous, telling myself that if her friend weren't there I would ask for her number, but that was just me trying to rationalize my fear. The truth is I was afraid Aaliyah wouldn't like me. My fears stopped me from doing anything, and I vowed that the next time I saw her, I would ask her out. But by then, she had a serious boyfriend. I'm not saying that if I had asked her out she would have become my girlfriend, but because I caved in to my fears and that voice of doubt, we will never know. Even if I wanted to, I couldn't even ask her out now because less than a year later she died in a tragic accident. You never know what tomorrow holds, so if you have an intuitive notion to do something, do it, and don't let fear stop you. I have fears just like you have fears. We all do. Our challenge is to move through them. We cannot let fear stop us from doing those dynamic things we are meant to do in our lives. Your life's journey is already laid out for you. It's your job not to let your fears stop you from anything.

Your fears—that voice of doubt—are what will try to make you passive, but if you move through it, you will find that you will build more momentum in all areas of your life to the point where you will catch fire. You'll be energized. You'll be vibrant. And what does that lead to? It leads to the ability to work hard and to work smart. And we already know where that leads. Today, just as a challenge, try doing one thing that scares you but would make your life better if you did it. Make a phone call you've been putting off, or sign up for a class you've wanted to take. Apply for a job you've been interested in, or try out for a team sport. Do the thing that frightens you. Do-

> *Do the thing that frightens you.*

ing the thing that frightens you is an *active* way to approach your life. You'll find that just by doing these things, no matter the result, you will be happier. Shaquille O'Neal believes, "Excellence is not a singular act, but a habit."

I have a friend here in Hollywood named Ron who every week seems to come up to me and tell me how he has these great ideas for movies or TV shows. Never once has Ron taken the action to actually write a movie or a show that he thinks is great, let alone produce or direct one. Ideas are just like that word "try"—" 'trying' to do something" or "I have this 'idea.'" Both mean nothing. It makes me want to yell, "Don't *try*. Just *do*." An idea is meaningless unless it is put into action. The only things that are important are truly putting ideas into action and following through—that's the doing-ness of life. Living a "doing life" means battling through your fears and doubts and actively pursuing all the things you want to do.

If you are being completely honest with yourself, doing those actions will lead you down the path toward MANifesting your destiny and unreasonable happiness. Start applying the doing-ness of life in *your* everyday life. I guarantee that great things will happen.

One last thing before I let you go. When we started writing letters back and forth, you promised me that you would start living according to the principles that we talk about. If you are holding up your end of that deal, then I never ever again want to hear you say that you are *trying* to do something. You and I, we will always *do* it. It's as simple as that.

All right now, talk to you soon. Hit me back. And do *your* thing today!

Your Friend,

Hill

----------Original Message----------

From: Young_Brotha@home.net
Date: February 3, 2006 9:45 PM
To: Hill@manifestyourdestiny.net
Subject: Gossip

Hill, why do people talk about other people all the time?

Date: February 4, 2006 11:43 AM
From: Hill@manifestyourdestiny.net
To: Young_Brotha@home.net
Subject: Re: Gossip

Just think about all of the entertainment TV shows and gossip magazines. Most people find the lives of those around them more interesting than their own. It seems a lot of folks would rather talk about others than themselves.

One reason people talk negatively about others is to take the focus off of how they really feel about their own lives. It is easier to turn other people's lives into entertainment than to admit our own fears and insecurities. Gossip may seem harmless, but talking bad about people just makes us feel worse about ourselves and never better like we expect. I recently learned that in Judaism, spreading rumors about other people is considered one of the worst sins you can commit. If you think about it, ruining someone's reputation can be almost as bad as killing them. Just like my grandfather used to tell me, "If you can't say something good about someone, boy, than you shouldn't say anything at all."

HH

Part Five

Winning at Your Life: Setting Sail

MANifest Your Destiny

The Power of Belief

Like a child, I had always believed that nothing is impossible until it could be proven impossible.
DUKE ELLINGTON

February 21, 2006
Los Angeles

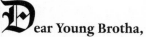ear Young Brotha,

In my last two letters I wrote to you about MANifesting your destiny and the doing-ness of life. Reading your response, especially the part where you talked about applying to Big Ten colleges, I can tell you have really embraced those principles. Now we need to talk about "belief" and "doubt." In order to MANifest your destiny, you must take action (doing-ness) and for that action to have an effect, you must believe. "First you believe it, and then you will see it." Believing is a necessary component to MANifesting your destiny and being unreasonably happy.

I'm reading this article in the Sunday *Parade* magazine

where Jamie Foxx talks about these very principles. Jamie said, "When I was growing up in Terrell, Texas, I felt that it was not where I was supposed to be. I knew that I was meant for a different destination. I think that the minute I was born, there was something inside telling me I would go far. It's like energy—an intangible destiny. And if you have someone to help clear your way ahead, it will take you where you're meant to go. . . . I'm not really here to make money. I want to make history. . . . I don't look around to see what others are doing. No, I see me." Wow! Talk about the power of belief. Jamie Foxx is a successful actor, musician, father, and Academy Award–winner, so he is living proof that these principles work. Ya heard?

> There is a power in faith and belief that is pure.

There is a power in faith and belief that is pure. It is transformational. Things happen in life that attempt to stomp that power out of us and so we stop believing. We stop trusting and stop knowing. Then there are things that confirm life to be divinely guided and perfect.

Unreasonable happiness is a happiness that makes no sense to the outside world, or even to you, at times. It is not dependent on outside circumstances or the approval of others. It just *is*. You are happy for no reason other than being and believing. Doubts are the main culprits of stealing that happiness away from us.

Some people call belief a "higher power," but you don't have to think about it that way. When most people say or think "higher power" it almost subconsciously distances them from that power source, as if it is unreachable. Belief—

true belief—is not at a distance from you. It is a part of you. It's already inside you. It's a part of every fiber of your being. Belief, true belief, is all around you and available to you all the time. So I call it my "alternative power" source. That means I have my very own source of power. It's mine. For instance, I have my own source of willpower, strength, and mental acuity (look it up), but I also have the alternative power. Alternative power is power that the universe that created me has given to me. Alternative power is like an outlet that is always plugged into the universe. There is no other person in the world exactly like I am. That means there is no other person in the world like you. There's a power in that. There is a power in that creation. It is the power of God. This power is everywhere: outside you, inside you, all around you, in everything you see, say, and do. This power is in every living breathing thing in the universe. It is always at your disposal and in infinite supply. And best of all, it's free; it doesn't cost any money. But, it is up to you to use it. You don't need to sign up. You don't need a computer, a perfect space, a professional sports contract, or anything other than yourself and a willingness to connect to this power. No matter how much money you do or don't have, you can always use this alternative power.

How do you do it, you ask? How do you use this free source of alternative power? How can it change your life for the better? Here's how. You take a moment to be alone. Sit quietly. Do this right now. It could be in your bedroom, it could be in the library, in a park, or at a bus stop. It doesn't matter where. Okay. I want you to imagine yourself, and in your imagination think of what you believe to be the best version of you: the version of you that you love the most. You get me on this? You're sitting there imagining the best version of you, in your "mind's eye," which means your imagination. Don't look outside yourself to see what others are thinking of you; this is an inner exercise. So go ahead, right now, imagine your "best self" saying hello to you right now.

I want you to be careful as you do this, because these days people have begun to confuse the "best" version of themselves with the "richest" most "bling-bling" version of themselves. I promise you that that is not truth. That's not what we're talking about here. Platinum Rolexes and Bentleys with twenty-inch chrome rims are often owned by people who, deep down, feel the least about themselves. They have to make themselves "feel" more important and valuable by adorning themselves with shiny, expensive, things. Now, I'm not saying there's anything wrong with having nice things. I know enough people who drive Bentleys and live behind gated estates who are not enslaved by their material trappings. I have nice cars myself. But, anytime you feel like you need a really expensive thing, you've gotta ask yourself the question, "Why do I feel like I 'need' to have this or that?" "Who am I trying to impress?" "Am I buying this thing because deep down I don't feel like I am enough?"

Remember that by "best self" I mean the version of you at this moment that is the most unreasonably happy, dynamic, energized, vibrant, and fun. Oh and here's a hint, your "best self" will continually evolve. Year after year, month after month, you will expand and become more. Look at Dr. Dre, who said, "Even

> **Your "best self" will continually evolve.**

when I was close to defeat, I rose to my feet." His best self changed over the course of his entire career. He started out as a rapper with NWA, and his best version of himself today is not that of a rapper but as a producer for people like Eminem and 50 Cent. Take Malcolm X: He started out as part of the Nation of Islam and then he broke away because his best self evolved into someone he felt could be most effective working outside of a particular organized religious group. Or take Tupac for instance. He began as an actor at a performing arts school, and then found that he enjoyed music and started rapping. Tupac was always politically involved and found that he could be most effective by weaving messages of political change into the music he created. All three of these men are prime examples of believing in themselves, working hard, and working smart, passionately representing their "best selves" to the world.

I hope you continue to explore connecting to the alternative power of belief that is at your disposal all the time through your imagination. The coolest thing about this power is that the more you connect to it, the more you believe, and on and on. This belief will build on itself within you and create a momentum, a centrifugal force, that will start to permeate every action you take in life. Another method I use to connect to that power is to write myself notes and leave them around my crib. I even stick them on the dashboard of my car, on the mirror in my bathroom, and on my bedside table. I call these notes "affirmations," and they say stuff like, "You will make today a great day." "You will be positive and passionate all day." And "You will kick butt on the track team and set a new personal best time." If you think this is corny, just try it. Affirmations work, I'm telling you. They help you to believe in yourself—try it today. To take affirmations to the next level, there's a tool I use called "vision into being." But we'll talk more about that later.

OK, I'm gonna go take on this day. It's going to be a great one. I hope you are as excited about our letter exchange as I am. It is good to have a friend like you. Hit me back or e-mail soon. Be well, my Brotha.

Your Friend,

Hill

----------Original Message----------

From: Young_Brotha@home.net
Date: February 25, 2006 4:47 PM
To: Hill@manifestyourdestiny.net
Subject: Making Money

Hill, what's a quick way to make money?

Date: February 27, 2006 2:38 PM
From: Hill@manifestyourdestiny.net
To: Young_Brotha@home.net
Subject: Re: Making Money

Okay, first of all, I know you don't want to hear this, but there is no quick way to make money that is legal.

Making "quick money" is not what I want you to be aspiring to, anyway. I want you to aspire to being wealthy (if money is what you want) because wealth is having a *whole lot* of money. For instance, Bill Gates did not make "quick money," but he is extremely wealthy. His net worth is so large he makes Diddy look broke. Building long-term wealth from creating something valuable or providing a service is much better than "quick money." By definition "quick money" is small money. And like Jay-Z says: "Come see me when your bank account grows up." It can't grow up "quick." It takes time.

So, the best way to wind up with a lot of money is to always have a job (income) and every week save a tiny bit of that money that's coming in. That weekly savings will grow exponentially and turn into real wealth. Regular saving works over time. Trust me!

HH

Vision into Being

Reality is wrong. Dreams are for real.
TUPAC

March 15, 2006
Hawaii!

Dear Young Brotha,

I'm writing back to you from Hawaii. I really wanted to hit the sand and surf for a minute before going back to work. A little vacation and quiet time is never a bad thing. Everyone needs to take time to reflect.

Your letter is so full of questions responding to my last letter about "the power of belief." But the one question that stood out the most was, "Hill, how do I begin doing something when I cannot even imagine myself doing it?" That's a great question. But you know what? I got an answer.

Do you remember in my last letter, I told you that there was this thing I call "vision into being"? Some people call it "visualization," which means holding a vision in your mind until you can see, touch, and taste it—until it is so real the universe has no choice but to bring it into reality. Some people even call that "pretending." Now, I know that sounds odd, but I'm gonna explain it to you. Ya see, it's so easy for all of us to pretend. In fact, many of us spend most of our lives pretending to be something that we really aren't or pretending to feel some way that we really don't. Whenever someone says, "I'm just keepin' it real," that's the first clue that they're pretending. Because when you're really "keepin' it real" you never need to say it. It's obvious to everyone that you are. What I'm talking about here is different from "pretending." It's about believing in something so strongly that you conspire with the energy of the universe to make it real. I call it "Vision into Being."

Jim Carrey has a legendary story about the power of visualization I'm talking about. When he was a struggling comic he decided that one day he would become a rich, successful actor. So he took out his checkbook and he wrote himself a check for ten million dollars. At the time, he barely had a hundred dollars in his account, let alone ten million. But every day Jim Carrey carried that check inside his wallet. It allowed his mind to visualize that he would be able to go to the bank one day and cash it. He continued to work very hard honing his craft; believing. Believing in the power of visualization, he had faith that one day he would be able to walk into the bank and cash that check. Vision into Being is such a powerful tool that since that day he wrote the check he has earned way more than he initially set out to earn. While he was struggling, if he had told someone he was carrying around a ten million dollar check made out to himself, they would have laughed in his face. By sharing this information before his dream happened, it would have destroyed the power because it would have al-lowed someone else to project fear onto his dream. That is why when you use the power of visualization, you must keep it to yourself until your dream is made MANifest. Today Jim Carrey commands twenty million dollars a movie. How is that for Vision into Being? But remember, Jim Carrey had to continue to work extremely hard pursuing his dream. He didn't just sit back and pretend that that check would be cash-able without him working hard.

So you say you want to get an A on your Am. Lit. test? Do you see how visualization can help you? Commit to studying the way that you think the guy who wrote your Am. Lit. text-book studied when he was researching the information he needed to create the book. Remember, all that information in that textbook came out of someone's brain—someone's brain that is an older model. So therefore, write yourself a note that says, "I am going to get an A on my Am. Lit. test, and I will un-derstand the material as well as the author." Put that note in your pocket and read it to yourself at least once a day. Continue to study as test day approaches, having faith that the combination of your

I want you to be as powerful as you can be.

hard work and Vision into Being will yield the result you desire. It works. I promise. It's part of the same thing I explained to you when I said that there is power in believing and in visualization—these are all related. I want you to be as powerful as you can be. I want you to use every resource available to you.

Once there was this girl in high school who I had a huge crush on. Erin was hot, smart, successful, and a very giving person . . . and I was afraid to ask her out. I let my fear stop me from doing something that I really wanted to do. So, although I didn't call it that at the time, I decided to use Vision into Being. I kept a brand new silver dollar inside my pocket and decided it made everything that I said funny and cool. I believed that if I stuck my hand inside my pocket and touched that silver dollar it gave me those powers. Truly believing gave me a confidence that was already inside me, and so I asked her out. And guess what? She became my girlfriend.

I can't stress enough that the power of Vision into Being is only for you. You don't need to argue or defend being right. Somebody else's vision and your vision may not be the same thing, and that's fine because we are talking about your journey here; your life, not theirs. The only person that needs to know you are right is you.

Vision into Being will give you more confidence. It will make you surer of yourself. It will make you stronger. It will make you less fearful. It does for me.

Hey, I gotta go now. The waves are just right, and I'm learning how to surf. I know what you're thinking and yes, brothers can surf. (And you know I love learning new things!) Be well my friend. My next letter to you is going to be about wealth and winning and what each really means. Hit me back, or e-mail me. I'll check my e-mails from the hotel. ALOHA!

Your friend,

Hill

----------Original Message----------

From: Young_Brotha@home.net
Date: March 23, 2006 9:07 PM
To: Hill@manifestyourdestiny.net
Subject: Life

Hill,

Why does it feel like life is so hard for me sometimes?

Date: March 24, 2006 8:59 AM
From: Hill@manifestyourdestiny.net
To: Young_Brotha@home.net
Subject: Re: Life

First of all, you are not alone. Life feels that way for *everybody* at times no matter how old you are, no matter where you live, no matter what you do. Every day we are faced with challenges and choices. Some are harder than others. And sometimes, what seems like a big deal at the time doesn't matter at all a week later. The one thing I've learned is that if I approach each day with an attitude of gratitude, even the most difficult challenges fail to bring me down.

It's often harder when you're younger because many decisions are made for you and there are many rules to follow, but your attitude can still make a big difference. Be patient and know that if you can make it through today, tomorrow's challenges and choices may be a lot easier.

But on this question in particular I want you to have the perspectives of someone younger than me and a peer from Harvard, one of the most intelligent men I know. So I e-mailed Ray J and Barack Obama and asked them to respond to your question. Ray J's song *One Wish* was one of the number-one releases of 2006, but don't think it's always been easy for him. He is a great talent and an amazing young man, but we all experience ups and downs. The honorable Barack Obama is a friend from Harvard Law School, and is a senator from Illinois. Here's what these two inspiring men wanted you to know, Young Brotha:

----------Begin Forwarded Message----------

Being Ray J today is not as hard as it once was. Even though I came from a good home, I often chose my own way. I really didn't have a reason to hang out with the wrong crowd but I did anyway—just rebellious, young, and trying to find myself, like most teenagers. One day when I almost got shot in front of my house, my grandma, and my family, I realized it was no more fun and games. This event forced me to reevaluate my life before I lost it. It wasn't easy, but my family was there to support me and I was determined to do positive things. I still got love for my experiences because they have helped me become who I am today, and are daily reminders of what life could have been. Life is not always easy and there is always struggle but in the end I appreciate what I have based on what I have overcome.

Stay Strong,
Ray J

----------Begin Forwarded Message----------

Dear Young Brother,

Life appears to be hard sometimes because life *is* hard sometimes. None of us have control of the circumstances into which we are born. We may be born into poverty, we may be born in a country filled with strife and torn by war. We may even confront the failings of our own parents. For African-Americans in this country, we have additional hurdles to overcome—the legacy of slavery and Jim Crow, and the ongoing problems of discrimination.

Despite all that, your life is what you make it. Those who achieve don't waste time on self-pity. They don't spend time focused on how unfair life is. They don't blame other people for their problems and they don't use race or poverty or hardship as an excuse for failure. Instead they strive for excellence. They take responsibility for their actions and they try to focus on not just themselves, but on others. In fact, when you focus on others you realize the blessings you have—like the man complaining he had no shoes until he saw a man with no feet. There are many people in the world who have far fewer opportunities than you do.

It doesn't mean that you can't get down sometimes. Everybody does. But, always remember that being defeated is a temporary condition. Giving up is what makes it permanent.

Barack

Wealth and Winning

Only dumb people try to impress smart people. Smart people
just do what they do.
CHRIS ROCK

April 4, 2006
Los Angeles

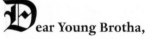ear Young Brotha,

Hey, it just hit me. It's been almost a year since I received your first letter, which is amazing. It feels like I've known you forever.

And congratulations! You worked hard and smart and utilized the power of Vision into Being and you got an A on that Am. Lit. test. That A is an example of how *wealthy* you are. I know you're like, "Hill, I got an A on a test; it didn't pay me any money." And you're right, getting an A on your test didn't pay, but that doesn't mean that it's not an example of how wealthy you are.

I'm about to say something that is going to make you

crack up. I promise. Okay, here goes. You and I—both of us—
are wealthy beyond measure. Literally. Seriously. For real. We
are billionaires *already*. I know you're laughing right now saying, "I'm not a billionaire. I don't know about you Hill, but
I'm not." Well, if you looked at my bank account you'd see
that I'm not a billionaire either, not in terms of the dollars in
my account, but here's the deal. Life is all about definitions.
How you define something is critical. For instance, when we
talk about "wealth," we have to define what "wealth" is. It
needs to be our own personal definition.

If you embrace the wealth you already have, it will expand
into every area of your life—a loving family, good health, tal-

> *If you embrace the wealth you
> already have, it will expand
> into every area of your life.*

ent, a truly compas-
sionate spirit. I used to
have no clue how valu-
able all those things are.
When I first moved to
Hollywood, I needed a
job. I waited tables in a
twenty-four hour diner from eleven at night until seven in the
morning, so that I would be available during the day to audi-
tion for acting jobs. The busboys and kitchen staff nick-
named me Zapato, which means "shoe" in Spanish, because
my first night on the job my feet kept getting in the way as
they tried to clean the floor. The nickname stuck. One of the
busboys, Hector, noticed I was down about not having any
money and he sat me down one day. He said, "Zapato, come
here. I need to talk to you." We sat in a corner booth of the
restaurant at five in the morning. I could tell he was worried
about me. He said, "Don't get down, man. If you can wake
up each day and do your best to be a good person and stay
happy, then you will know what it is to be truly wealthy. All

the time people come in, and they ask to sit at your tables because you make them happy. That is a gift. That is worth so much more than money. You cannot always look in someone's wallet to know how wealthy they really are." He finished by saying, "What I have noticed most about you is that the greatest gift that God has given you is the ability to work harder than anyone that I know. That ability is worth more than a few dollars in your pocket." When I left the restaurant that morning I had only a few tips in my pocket, but his words made me realize how wealthy I truly was.

Wealth comes from knowing both your value in the world, as well as the value of the blessings life has brought you—family, friends, future opportunities, health, and the opportunity for true unreasonable happiness. You win when you embrace all of these and look toward the future with a positive attitude. So yes, you are wealthy *already* if you just look around you. And yes, like we've already talked about in previous letters, you can and will win at life, and here's how: Stay in the game, work hard and work smart, dream big, live with passion, MANifest your destiny, work past your fear, believe with conviction, and stay committed to the doing-ness of life. If you do all of these things, you can't help but win. And that's just the beginning of your wealth.

Your wealth in life is made up of a number of components, or important pieces. To give you an example, I'll break down the key wealth components in my life. The first key wealth component for me is good health. See, there's no way I can win in any area of my life unless I have the wealth of health as a starting point. A few years ago, doctors found that I had a tumor near my thyroid in my neck. They didn't know if it was cancer or not, and luckily for me, after doing multiple tests and biopsies, they determined that it wasn't cancerous, but I have to get it checked every six months. Without health, all of our great plans and future goals are meaningless. That is why the choices we make regarding whether to drink alcohol or smoke cigarettes or do drugs need to be governed by putting our health first. I don't smoke. It's not because I judge it as some "bad" thing; I choose not to smoke because I know that my father smoked, and he died of cancer, and my grandfather smoked, and he died of cancer. Those signposts in my past make it clear that it would be an extremely irresponsible and unhealthy choice for me to smoke. Same goes for drinking and driving, unprotected sex, or even eating too much fat and sugar without regularly exercising. So my definition of wealth is having the knowledge that I am healthy and happy enough to enjoy all of the experiences this incredible world offers me. If that is my definition of wealth, then I, along with my family and friends—which now includes you—am wealthy beyond measure. We are all billionaires ten times over. 'Cause now, just by virtue of us exchanging letters, you're part of my tribe. My tribe is exceedingly wealthy and unreasonably happy. That shows that we are committed to being winners. Your health is a key wealth component.

> **We are all billionaires ten times over.**

What do you think some other key wealth components are for you? Come on, think. What about your mind? Cultivating my mind and my ability to be a critical thinker has been enormously valuable to me in all areas of my life. People often say to me, "Don't you think it was a waste of time and money going to Harvard Law School? And you became an actor? So you don't even use it at all?" They are so wrong. Harvard Law School helped me to develop my mind. It helped strengthen my ability to communicate and to analyze information. All of these skills serve me greatly as an actor as well as in all areas of my everyday life. My ability to be a critical thinker is another wealth component that is crucial to me; it gave me valuable life skills. Are you a critical thinker? Do you want to develop that skill set?

Another wealth component for me is my spirituality and relationship with God, which I am immeasurably grateful for. God and the universe provide us with clues on how to walk our walk here on Earth. God provides us with clues on how to evaluate and make difficult choices we are faced with all the time. It is through my intuition that I notice God's guidance the most. My intuition is my open hotline to God, and being able to be patient and quiet enough to hear the messages that come through my intuition is an essential part of that God-given wealth component. I have found that daily prayer and meditation are effective tools in clearly hearing my intuition and understanding the messages that God sends me through that passageway. The ability to hear these messages is a true wealth component.

In addition to those wealth components, another essential component of being a true winner is learning to lose gracefully, because often losing is the universe's way of leading you toward your destiny. When I played football, I hated losing. If my team lost, I couldn't get rid of the feeling of defeat for days. I would shut off from everything and everyone. Even today, I have to force myself to stay in the game when something doesn't go my way. I actively use the tools I am sharing with you: meditation, visualization, staying in the game, working hard at working smart, believing, and living with passion.

For instance, two years ago I got a series regular job on a television show called *The Handler*, starring opposite Joe Pantoliano. When we were placed on the fall schedule, I was excited because I had regular work, which means fewer auditions, a weekly salary, and a character I was excited about playing. It was a dream job for an actor. I even bought a new house. I loved the work environment, my coworkers, and my character, and all of us became an extended family. It was perfect. Then, the ratings came in, and they were not as high as the network had been expecting. After sixteen episodes, we were told the show was going to be canceled. I was devastated. I was unemployed, again. I counted this as a huge loss. But guess what happened? Two weeks later, my agents called me about another series, called *CSI: NY*. It seemed that the creators of *CSI: NY* were familiar with my work on *The Handler* and were interested in meeting with me. I got the job. And now I am a part of one of the most successful franchises in the history of television. By my being on a show that wasn't a hit, other people who work in television became familiar with my work, and it led to an amazing job offer. It was the universe at work helping me to MANifest my destiny. If *The Handler* hadn't been canceled when it was, I wouldn't have been available to do *CSI: NY*. Unknown to me the universe conspired to help me win.

> The universe conspires
> to help you win.

As you proved in acing your Am. Lit. test, you, too, can win. And it's important to realize that what winning is for you may be different than what winning is for me, just like our definitions of wealth may be different. What would make you unreasonably happy may be different than what makes me unreasonably happy. For example, I get fan mail from people all the time who write to me saying, "This must be the happiest moment of your life to finally be on a hit TV show," or, "You must have been so happy the day you graduated from Harvard *cum laude*, with two graduate degrees." Yes, those fans are right; it's great to be on a hit show and to have gotten such prestigious degrees. However, as I look back, neither of those things are necessarily the "happiest moments" of my life.

Surprisingly, one of the happiest moments of my life so far happened when I was in high school. I was selected to play on an all-star football team called the Optimist Team. It was for a charity and made up of the best players from around the entire city. I'll never forget the call asking me to join the team. When I hung up the phone, I felt like I was floating on air. That, to me, was perhaps the most unreasonably happy moment of my life. For most people, they would say being on TV in front of millions of people every week is much better than playing on a high school football team. But that's the beauty of life: We all have individual and personal definitions of what winning is and what makes us happy. It's up to you to figure out and to be totally honest with yourself about what winning and wealth mean to you, and what being victorious and unreasonably happy in your life would look like.

Would a strong successful family be a "win" for you? Would having tons of options because you have an incredible education be a "win" for you? Would good health for you and your family and friends be a "win" for you? Would volunteering to help the homeless? Owning a professional basketball team? What?

What in your life, year-to-year, month-to-month, day-to-day, hour-to-hour, minute-to-minute, makes you unreasonably happy? Know that the definition of "winning" for you will change as your journey changes. That means that what you consider a "win" will change as you walk through life. For instance, if I got called today to play on an all-star football team, it probably wouldn't make me as happy as it did when I was in high school. But that's cool—life is a journey.

Define for yourself, right now, today, at this point, what winning would be. Would it be getting another A on your test tomorrow? Would it be writing your first novel? Would it be buying your mother a home? Would it be kissing the girl you have a crush on? What about throwing the winning pitch in a baseball game? Right now, in this moment, what would make you unreasonably happy? Whatever it is, know this: You can have it. You can achieve it. You can win. But to do that, you have to believe you can.

When you are "wealthy" in all aspects of your life, you are a winner.

Hey, I gotta run. I'm going to an awards party, and I told my man Ludacris I was going to be there. I know you like his song "Roll Out," so I'll send you a picture of him and me. Cool? Grace, Peace, and Blessings. One.

Your Friend,

Hill

---------Original Message----------

From: Young_Brotha@home.net
Date: April 12, 2006 10:13 PM
To: Hill@manifestyourdestiny.net
Subject: Mantras????

Hill, you told me to think about doing "mantras" and "affirmations."
But I can't come up with any. What are some I can do?

Date: April 13, 2006 11:21 AM
From: Hill@manifestyourdestiny.net
To: Young_Brotha@home.net
Subject: Re: Mantras????

Mantras and affirmations are strong tools that have been used for
thousands of years in prayer and meditation. They are related to
believing and having faith that you will achieve whatever you can
visualize or articulate for your future. They should always be positive statements referring to something you can make happen in
your life. It's funny, I got your e-mail the same day I was in a car
dealership. And the salesman I was talking to had some mantras
on his wall. He said that he reads them to himself every day, and
he thinks they help him maximize his potential. He calls them
"promises to himself." They were inspired by Gary Takacs who is a
highly respected business consultant. These are all great things
you can say to yourself on a daily basis.
  I promise:

- To be strong so that nothing can disturb my peace of
  mind.
- To make everyone feel that there is something special in
  them.

- To look at the positive side of everything and make my optimism come true.
- To be just as enthusiastic about the success of others as I am about my own.
- To learn from the mistakes of the past and press on to the greater achievements of the future.
- To have a cheerful presence at all times and give every living creature I meet a smile.
- To give so much time and effort to the improvement of myself that I have no time to criticize others.
- To be too large for worry, too noble for anger, too strong for fear, and too happy to permit the presence of trouble.
- To be a light for others, not a judge of others.

I taped these up on my mirror to remind me of these promises to myself. Mantras, affirmations, positive visualization, and belief all have power. Use that power. It is God's gift to you, and it's free.

HH

Final Letter:
The Wind
at Your Back

May you always swim in the ocean of abundance
manifesting your own divine destiny. Listen My friend.
RUMI

April 20, 2006
Los Angeles

ear Young Brotha,

In your most recent letter to me, you said that it was going
to be the last one for awhile because you already have so
much stuff to think about and put into practice from our previous letters. Just by you telling me this proves you have
grown wiser already. You realize that putting lessons into action is more important than continually coming up with
more and more lessons. You're right. If we don't put the lessons into action, they are meaningless.

The reason why I chose to quote Rumi above is because
he was a powerful spiritual philosopher, visionary, and poet
whose wisdom, even though he lived eight hundred years

ago, still enlightens millions of people today. Exchanging these letters with you has reconfirmed for me that there is an "ocean of abundance" in each of our lives. Our friendship is a part of that abundance. That's what you have become to me: a true friend. I want to listen to you and to be there for you as you grow and mature. Now the tables have turned, and I'm the one who has joined your fan club, The Young Brotha Fan Club. And I know that as you continue to practice the power of these lessons, that fan club will expand.

Before we stop exchanging letters regularly, I have two final challenges for you; two final things I want you to start practicing. They are: to be more *relaxed* and more *courageous* every day. So, each day, I want you to relax a little more . . . a little more . . . a little more. How? Every day, decide that you are going to take fewer (but deeper) breaths than you took the day before. I try to begin each morning when I wake up by saying a prayer and taking a few deep breaths while thinking about all the great potential that this one day—today—holds. Because yesterday is gone and tomorrow ain't here yet, today is the only day that really matters. I breathe deeply and relax into the day ahead.

I want you to breathe deeper and deeper and deeper. To do that you'll have to consciously and with intent practice taking deeper breaths every day. Try it now. Breathe as deep as you can right now. Fill your lungs up with air as far as they will go. Okay. So now you know how much air you can take in today. Each day, by breathing deeper and deeper, you will be a little bit more relaxed, which will help you "re-act" less and therefore "act" more relaxed and courageous. Do you see what I'm saying? The more you are relaxed the less you will be reactive. Most bad, negative things that happen to young people are usually not because of their "actions" but because of their "re-actions." Someone does something or says something you take personally, and you react. Your mom or pop makes you feel a certain way, and you react. The clerk at the grocery store looks at you funny, and you react.

"Actions" without the "re" are much more about courage, and courageous action is just like any muscle: You have to develop it. Like going to the gym, the more you use a muscle, the stronger it will get. The more courageous actions you take, the stuff that used to take courage—like telling someone "I love you" or supporting and helping the least popular kid in school—will become easy. The happiest and most successful people in the world have one thing in common: They Act With Courage. They take risks. I hope that in this next year, you will take more risks than you have taken in your entire life up until now.

> *I hope that in this next year, you will take more risks than you have taken in your entire life up until now.*

It is your duty once you have embraced these lessons and have begun to MANifest your destiny that you pass on what you have learned in your journey to your younger brothas. Once you set your intention to teach these lessons to someone willing and eager to benefit from them, the universe will place people in your path the same way you were placed in mine. Remember, helping others allows the universe to pour forth more blessings into your own life, so ultimately both you and your younger brotha win, and that's what we are—winners.

Over the course of this last year, you have graduated from

being a boy into becoming a man, and it has been an honor to witness your growth. We have developed a bond that I know is going to be with me for the rest of my life, and I hope you feel the same. It has been a blessing and an honor to exchange these letters with you. I hope you don't think that what I am about to say is corny, but, *I love you* Young Brotha. I mean that. I choose my friends as if they are family, and you are now *my family*.

There is someone that I've recently learned about, and the more I hear about his spirit, the more he reminds me of you. His name was Nkosi Johnson. Nkosi was born with AIDS in South Africa. He lived only until the age of twelve, but during his short life he worked tirelessly on behalf of other children with AIDS, insisting that every child is important. At twelve years old, he became a strong and vibrant voice for a disadvantaged and largely ignored group of people. He was a fighter. A revolutionary. He made the world take notice of the health crisis that was going on in his country by being a fierce activist and speaking out against injustice. After his death, Nelson Mandela spoke about him. He said: "Nkosi Johnson was an icon of the struggle for life for millions of people in Africa and the world. He was a young man of infinite *courage* who gained wisdom far beyond his years on the planet."

I'd like to share with you an amazing quote Nkosi Johnson offered the world before he passed away. This twelve-year-old "MAN" said: "Do what you *can*, with what you *have*, in the *place* you are, with the *time* you have *left*." If a young man with only twelve years on the planet can affect millions of people worldwide, just imagine the impact you will be able to have over the course of your lifetime. This just goes to show you that you can achieve anything you set your intention to achieve. Anything! Isn't that amazing? All of this life, your life, is down this wondrous path before you. The journey, your journey, begins right now. This second. This moment. With each blink of your eye you are farther down your path.

I'm sad that we won't be corresponding as often as we have, but I'm also excited to see and bear witness to the MAN you are becoming. You are a true friend and a fellow traveler on this journey called life. Stay strong. Stay humble. Stay compassionate, and never settle. Be a man who is relaxed, intelligent, compassionate, acts courageously, loves unconditionally, and let your life reflect that truth.

I wish you Unreasonable Happiness. And you know something? I *know* you will have it. Your Destiny is Glorious, MANifest It. Our letters and e-mails have been about you taking your life to the next level and living it to its fullest capacity. This, right now, is your opportunity—the wind is at your back, and I want to see you FLY!

Be well my friend. Be well, my Young Brother!

Your Friend and Brother,

Hill Harper

Acknowledgments

God is the creator of all things, and when it comes to expressing the gratitude in my heart, for me, that's where it begins.

The creation of this book has been divinely guided, and I would like to thank those individuals who helped shape my vision into these pages. My publisher and editors at Gotham Books: William Shinker, Lauren Marino, and Hilary Terrell. My incredibly supportive book team: Stephanie Covington; Danielle DeJesus; Margaret Dunlap; Keith Major; Voltaire Sterling; Darrell Smith; David Vigliano; Elisa Petrini; Lisa Sorensen; Guy Dunn, Jr.; Jesse Shane; Dylan Chapman; my aunt, Ercelle Pinckney; and my mother, Marilyn Hill Harper.

Heartfelt thanks to my friends and colleagues who

through their thoughtful e-mails in this book gave generously of their time and wisdom.

And special acknowledgement and thanks to Marvet Britto and everyone at The Britto Agency. Without championing this project from the beginning, the book you see today would not have been possible.

And thanks to my friends, family, and ancestors who have always encouraged me to take risks, to live a life of unreasonable happiness, and to create works that seek to uplift the human spirit.

And finally, thank-you to all of the teachers I have had throughout my life who have fostered in me a love of learning, including those spiritual teachers who have shown me the importance and necessity of taking God along on my journey.

Also by Hill Harper

In his first book for adults, *New York Times* bestselling author Hill Harper invites you to join the Conversation: an honest dialogue about the breakdown of African-American relationships.

The *New York Times* bestselling book of inspirational advice and wisdom for young women from the powerhouse public speaker, star of *CSI: NY*, and bestselling author of *Letters to a Young Brother*

Available now wherever books are sold

GOTHAM BOOKS